Asleep *Wheel* at the

Taking Back Control of Your Life

Author: Marcus Black

Published by Cedar Gate Publishing, Contact Holden Hill or Randy Allsbury

Copyright © 2020 Marcus Black

Cover Design: Scott Soliz, www.zealdesino.com

Transcription Editor: Cindy Strickland

Revisions: Marcus Black

Content Editor: Darnell Blake

Line Editor: Emily Rucker

ISBN-13: 978-0999711736

Library of Congress Control Number: 2020933692

DEDICATION

To: Rachel Raquel Black. My dearest bride, best friend, and partner in life. Without you, this book wouldn't be possible. Thank you for listening to all of my wild ideas about writing this book for well over 10 years. Thank you for being my number 1 fan, my biggest cheerleader, and for believing in me, even when I didn't believe in myself. Most importantly, thank you for finally telling me to stop talking to you about the book until I started taking steps to make this dream a reality. I love you Forever & Always!

To my two boys, Marcus Dewayne II & Greyson Aundra. You two boys have made me the luckiest man alive. I'm so blessed to be your father. Sometimes, this life can be cruel and very hard to handle at times. We all struggle and find ourselves a little off track. Should either of you find yourselves in this place, no matter what happens to me or where this life takes you, may you both always find my voice in this book, leading you back to life, love, passion, and purpose. Keep dreaming! Keep growing! Keep living and loving life, Because YOU CAN!

To my beautiful twin and mother Pamela, my biggest supporter and dad Wayne, and my first two best friends and brothers Victor and Julius, I love you all dearly and may these words bring new life and encouragement to your hearts always!

And to all of my extended family, friends, and every person who I've ever come into contact with that has shown love, supported me, encouraged me, and helped me along the way, this is for you!! May the words invest as much in you as you have into me!

CONTENTS

FOREWORD

I t's amazing how quickly it happens. I've been there. You've been there. We all have. We've all been going about our daily lives just fine, and out of nowhere, sleep creeps in like a predator stalking its prey. Many times, we never even see it coming. It sneaks up on us and the next thing we know, we find ourselves slowly drifting away. I know there was a time in my life where I was on top of the world. After a stellar career at Baylor University, I finally achieved my lifelong dream of being signed and playing in the NFL. I was getting everything I ever wanted, and I had plans to become one of the greatest to ever play the game. That's when it happened to me. I remember it like it was yesterday. I was cut from my first NFL team.

This was a major strike to my pride and my ego. I would eventually get another shot a few short weeks later only to have my dreams snatched away from me again. I wasn't cut because I didn't perform well enough. It actually was quite the opposite. I was one of the rookie leaders in several statistical categories in the preseason and performing well amongst my peers. I was cut because I had sustained a knee injury that kept me from being fully available to my team. I wish I could tell you this was the last time I would experience this heartbreak, but unfortunately this was just the beginning of the end for my NFL career. After this moment, my dream of dominating the National Football League quickly began to turn into a nightmare.

From this point, I wound up in a cycle of being cut, signed, and cut again by several teams around the league. This left a giant-sized hole in my heart, and I slowly began to drift off my path in this life. I began to make bad choices and create new destructive habits in order to attempt to fill the void left in my heart. My life was in shambles, and I wasn't being a man. I was pointing the finger and blaming everyone else rather than accepting responsibility for my own choices. This new reality began to cause worry, doubt, and depression to set in, and I drifted off at the wheel of my life!

It was at this point in my life when something Miraculous happened! God blessed me with one of the greatest gifts I could ever receive in the birth of my first child, Tristan. This was the first of two major events in my life that forced me to rise up and become the man you know and love today. The second major event was when my college roommate and one of my closest friends committed suicide. These two events served as my wakeup call in life and motivated to create Rehab Time! My wakeup call literally opened my eyes, and together they pushed me down the path of passion, purpose, and impact that you know me for today.

Maybe you can relate to these feelings I shared above. Maybe your story, like mine, is filled with past hurt, pain, heartache, and disappointment. Perhaps you've taken one major loss in life after another. You once had all the zeal in the world, but life gets hard and has a way of really draining you and sucking you dry. Maybe you struggle with loving yourself, comparing yourself to others, and feeling unhappy and unfulfilled in life. From my own personal story, I get it. No one is exempt from having struggles in this life, and we've all grown tired and weary of the constant fighting for control of our lives.

If you've ever felt stagnant as if your life was on hold or any of the other feelings I mentioned above, that's exactly why you should read my good friend Marcus Black's book. If you've been looking for a book to spur you into the greatness you were created for, look no further. This is your wakeup call. Asleep at the Wheel is a compilation of very real, relevant, and heart felt stories that are guaranteed to give you the tools and formula you need to take back control of your life. Over the last year, I've grown to truly know Marcus' heart, and I can assure you that he is the perfect person to write this book because his deepest desire is serve, provide real world solutions, and to make a positive impact in your heart and life.

Should you find yourself struggling to take control of the wheel in your life, you've come to the right place. You didn't stumble upon this book by accident. This incredible work by my brother and friend is definitely going to impact your life in a positive way. Now, I hope you have your pen and pad ready because it's time to get to work. Let's get it!

Trent Shelton

Author, Speaker, and founder of Rehab Time

Chapter 1

ASLEEP AT THE WHEEL

Being a college student is not easy. Being a college student far away from home is even more difficult. You're out of your general comfort zone. You no longer have a safety net. You just have to figure it out. And so, you can imagine how difficult it was for me, being from a small suburban town in Mississippi, to relocate halfway across the country to Texas. I was away from my family, my support system, and everything I knew.

I love Texas and was able to establish a foundation in my life there. I met many wonderful people. I met the woman I married. We've been married for seven wonderful years now.

But college wasn't quite home. You know that feeling; there's just something about home that makes the heart sing. Because of this, I would often hop in my car on the spur of a moment and drive home. I would just get in the car and go since it was only about a seven-hour drive. I literally went home every two or three weeks sometimes.

I preferred to drive overnight because there was nobody else on the road except me and the 18-wheelers. It was amazing because you could get where you were going with no problems and little to no traffic.

There is one particular trip that I'll never forget. I had woken up at 6:00am after having gone to bed around 3:00am, so I was working on three hours of sleep. I spent my entire day running from one event to the next, mingling with friends and catching up with companions.

I was getting ready to head home for the holidays, so I hopped in my car around midnight just as I had done so many times before. Little did I know, I was about to experience one of the most significant moments of my life. The trip typically takes about five hours, from where I was in the Dallas area, to Little Rock, Arkansas. I hoped to reach this checkpoint around sunrise since it's the home stretch after that. I had done this drive many times before, and at first, this time was no different. I drove all night with no issues; I was moving and shaking, vibing out listening to music, and feeling great. You know that good feeling when you're in the car, wide awake, and the need to sleep doesn't hit you. Until it does.

That's what happened to me. Little did I know that I was getting ready to enter the fight of my life. My eyes began to get heavy, so heavy it felt like the weight of the world was resting on each eyelid. I was doing everything I could to fight it. I was slapping myself in the face. I was patting myself on the head and pinching myself as hard as I could. I let my windows down so the cold air would blow in my face, but my head kept nodding anyway. I was delirious and couldn't even see straight. But I kept fighting it and pressing on.

I'm sure you can relate to this feeling of utter exhaustion, where you can feel the need to sleep in your bones. It always seems to happen at the most inopportune times, too. I never get that feeling when I'm trying to relax and fall asleep at night. Instead, my brain likes to think it's in the Indy 500, racing a million miles an hour.

When it should be preparing to wind down it's busy thinking about every single decision that I have to make in life over the next year. It's contemplating what I'm going to eat the next day, where I'm going to go, my work projects, my wife and kids, and my goals. My brain won't stop. Unfortunately, the weight of the world doesn't rest on my eyelids in that moment and the need to sleep doesn't strike.

The unrelenting need to sleep seems to come to me when I'm driving or when I have somewhere important to be, somewhere where I need to be alert. The need to sleep often attacks when I'm in an important meeting with supervisors or maybe attending a presentation, times where I need to be alert in order to respect the people who are around me sharing their hearts with me. I know you can identify with this. And that's exactly where I was, trying to stay awake while driving. But that's not where I finished.

It'd be nice if I could tell you that was the end of my story that day. That I stopped and got some caffeine in me. That a jolt of energy and a second wind came to me and nothing happened. That it was a smooth ride the remainder of the way home. I wish I could tell you that's what happened, but unfortunately that's not the case.

What actually happened was my car slowly began to drift to the right. I had fallen asleep at the steering wheel while going 75 miles per hour on the interstate. The two passenger-side wheels of my car slowly crossed over the rumble strips that were put into place to be loud enough to startle someone if they were leaving the road. But in this instance, they didn't serve their purpose. I was completely asleep, and my wheels crossed over. My driver-side wheels also crossed over and my entire car slowly drifted from a position of safety in my lane on the interstate, heading toward my destination, to no longer being on the road at all.

I still didn't wake up. I'm not sure what got my attention, but my eyes popped open, only to see a guard rail about 15 feet in front of me. That's when everything seemed to go in slow motion. I woke up just in time to swerve back onto the highway and narrowly avoided a major catastrophe. My life was spared and my journey was forever altered.

Reflecting on this experience led me to a significant revelation. Nobody plans to fall asleep at the wheel. Nobody gets in a car with a destination in mind and says, "I think I'm just gonna take a nap while behind the wheel for a while." Nobody plans to do that. Nobody plans to take themselves from a place of safety, a place of purpose, or a path that leads to their destination. You don't plan to get a divorce the day you say "I do". You never plan to go broke and live in a constant state of financial crisis. You don't plan to be unhealthy or unhappy in this life. It just slowly happens over time as the weight of the pressures in this life mount up and cause you to become "sleepy." Nobody plans to step away from safety and security in order to move into the danger zone of falling asleep at the wheel.

But the sad reality is, the same way I fell asleep at the wheel on the interstate, in some area, you've fallen asleep at the wheel of your life. It didn't happen swiftly or overnight. It's entirely possible that you don't even know you're asleep. Maybe you're reading the words on this page and just now realizing that this may be your very own life. You slowly began to drift away from your passions. You slowly began to move away from your purpose and from the life that you loved to live, and now you find yourself trapped in the monotony of an unfulfilled life.

You feel stagnant as if you aren't moving forward towards your goals and dreams. You're going through the motions in your faith-walk. You're going through the motions in your finances, your family, or your fitness, and you don't know how you got here. You're truly unhappy, unfulfilled, and you're wondering where you went wrong. Wondering if it's ever going to be possible to find your way again in this life. If you've ever found yourself wrestling with any of these feelings, you're not alone. It's quite common for this to happen.

Maybe you find yourself in this place, or maybe there's some other area of your life that you once had control over that you now feel slipping through your grasp. You previously felt alive and well. You were born into this world with dreams, hopes, passions, the things you aspired to be. But now, somewhere along the way, you slowly began to lose control. You found yourself merely existing, asleep at the wheel. You're doing everything in your power to survive day after day. You want to be filled with life and purpose again.

All you want is to be filled with genuine passion for life again. You're tired of the alternative. You're sick and tired of being sick and tired. You feel empty almost daily, and you don't know what you're working toward. You feel unfulfilled because nothing satisfies that itch that's inside of you. You lost that part of you that wanted to dream, that wanted something great, and that knew you could accomplish anything. You're unhappy, and that unhappiness is ruining you and driving you into the ground, and you don't know which way to turn.

Perhaps you're in a stage of life right now where you have been blessed with much of what you've dreamed for. But for whatever reason, your current reality doesn't measure up to the vision you pictured in your mind for so many years. You're frustrated and possibly at the end of your rope. You feel like giving up. You feel hopeless and don't know which way to turn. You desperately need something, some catalyst, to step in and shake you up. To give you the way, give you the plan, give you the keys to make it your reality.

I am here to tell you today that it doesn't matter where you find yourself on this spectrum that we've just uncovered. It doesn't matter how asleep you are. This is not how your story ends. This is not the end of your life. You could be completely asleep at the wheel of your life going 75 miles per hour on the interstate just like I was. I can think of a million and one ways I could have, would have, should have died that day. My life flashed before my eyes. But I didn't run into an 18-wheeler. I didn't overcorrect. My car didn't flip. All the different things that could have happened, didn't.

No matter how bad it appeared to be, I am still here. And you, my friend, are still here too. Since you woke up today with a heart still beating in your chest, life still exists. Everything you ever wanted is still in front of you. Over the course of this book, we're going to go on a journey together to uncover the things you want most in life. I will help you wake up and take back control of the wheel of your life. It's time to truly live and love life, to go and build a fulfilling life filled with moments and memories to last you and your children's children a lifetime.

So, are you ready? Will you go on this journey with me? We have some work to do. It's time to build the life you love to live. Because YOU CAN.

Vital Reflections to Discuss or Journal:

1. *Reflect on your own life. In what area(s) of your own life have you fallen asleep at the wheel? List them out in detail.*

2. *How does this revelation make you feel?*

3. *We're getting ready to go on an incredible journey of purpose and self-discovery. What major changes do you want to see in your life after completing this book?*

Chapter 2

IT'S A HARD-KNOCK LIFE

Some of my fondest childhood memories revolve around a room full of friends, laughing, playing and having a blast with video games. They were a huge part of my life growing up. We played one game in particular thousands and thousands of times called *Street Fighter*. My dad would often come in and play with me and my friends, and I can still hear the screams of excitement and peals of laughter as we indulged in this game.

However, one day it all changed, and not for the better. That day is etched in my mind for all eternity. I had so much fun playing video games and being with friends that I never imagined it would eventually have such a negative effect on me. My dad had just gone to sleep because he had to work later that night. Like so many times before my friend and I were playing *Street Fighter*. We had played the game 30 or 40 times that day, and this time my friend won the match. My character died that special video-game death, and all I heard was his voice echoing as the character faded away and finally lay lifeless on the ground.

I can't fully explain what happened to me in that moment. All I can liken it to is being sucked into a vacuum. It felt like my life was leaving my body. It was like I zoomed out into this black space and everything around me was far away. All I could hear were voices echoing in my head. The hairs on my arms stood up and I couldn't breathe. I was hyperventilating and couldn't figure out what was happening to me. Then this extreme fear overcame me and hit me like a ton of bricks. I imagined my own lifeless body lying there suffocating in a box and being covered with dirt. It felt like I was being buried alive.

Seeing me, my friend began to panic. He ran out of the room and got my mom. As she frantically came into the room, it was like a sudden and mighty wind came in with her. Breath blew into my lungs and I snapped out of it, gasping for air. My mom rushed over while I continued trying to catch my breath, asking over and over, "Baby, baby, what's wrong?" Tears filled my eyes as I looked at my mom and asked, "Mommy, am I going to die?"

I remember her voice so vividly, as if her heart was being crushed into a million pieces to have to answer this question for her nine-year-old child far sooner than she would have liked to. She bent down, looked directly at me and said, "Son, yes, you are. You are going to die, but not for a very long time. So, you don't need to worry about that. It's going to be okay." She hugged me and consoled me, and slowly I began to work my way back into my normal state of being.

I'd love to be able to say that was the only time I ever had a bout with the monster that is known as anxiety. However, that was only the beginning. It was a frequent visitor during my childhood, and then throughout my life. Even to this very day it still finds ways to come back. It doesn't affect me the way it used to because I've found ways to battle it. But it is something that continues to come over and over and over again as a recurring, horrible nightmare in my life.

When I was younger, I catered my entire state of being to this extreme fear that had first appeared when I was a small child. The thought of losing my senses, my family and those I love… that terrified me. The thought of losing my life crippled me. As a Christ-follower, I was taught from an early age that I had nothing to fear in the after-life because of a strong foundation built on my faith. You might be asking yourself, then, "If you believe you know what exists beyond this life, why are you so fearful?" Even though I know in my heart what happens after I pass, that wasn't enough to stop this monster from perpetually coming to visit me throughout the years.

This led me to an awareness in my life - far earlier than I would have liked for it to come. That realization is that life is hard. Life is difficult for a number of reasons. Maybe you can identify with the story I just shared. Maybe you can't, but nevertheless, you have your own story. Your story may be filled with grief and loss. Maybe it's filled with neglect and hurt. Maybe you've suffered from deeply broken relationships or extreme financial hardships. Perhaps you were taken advantage of. We live in a sad, unfortunate world where evil exists. There are sexual predators who attack the very innocence of a child, and maybe you find yourself in that place where your innocence was taken away from you and it hurts.

Your personal story has led you to the same realization that I discovered at a young age. It's a hard knock life. It's even more difficult because it doesn't come with an instruction manual. It would be so much easier if life came with this wonderful book that we all opened up as small children. It could have told you how to handle that school bully on the playground that wanted to belittle you and take away your joy in life and your dreams. Imagine if there was a manual to prepare you for the loss of your best friend or a loved one and all the grief that your heart would be overcome with. The sad reality, though, is there's nothing to prepare you for that.

There's nothing to prepare you to watch someone you love or deeply care about suffer from a great sickness, one that can take their life from them. It transforms your entire life. You end up living in and out of hospitals or hotels, fighting for your life, trying to survive and keep your family afloat despite all the medical bills. And I wish that there was a manual that could prepare you for the abuse that you went through in a negative relationship, having your heart broken while watching a parent being abused and then finding yourself repeating the same cycle in your own life.

Unfortunately, there are no manuals to help you overcome the evil that we so readily see every single day at the click of our fingertips. Being bombarded with evil and hatred and all of these things leads us to one place. It leads us to a place where we hope less. We become hopeless because we wonder, 'What is there to hope for anymore? Where can we find hope when there's so much difficulty, negativity, hurt, and evil in life?' Again, life hits you, and when it does it's so hard for you to see

ʹut. These things lead you to that slow fade that ː earlier that gradually veers you off your path a ___ ʋιt more and a little bit more until you come to the point of even wondering, 'What's the point?'

Maybe you find yourself at the end of your rope and you're ready to throw in the towel. You're ready to give up because you don't see the point of going on. You know there are people who love you, but you can't help it. You hear all the time what a selfish thing it is to in the towel and you feel grief in your heart for even allowing yourself to think about giving up. But that doesn't change the feelings you have inside as you wonder, 'Why should I even go on?'

I know you've felt this way because those were the very thoughts that I had in my own heart over the years as I allowed my life to be riddled with the fear of dying. What I finally came to understand was that I had ordered so much of my life around this extreme monster that I imagined was coming to take my life, that I was no longer living my life. I sacrificed things that I loved to do, things that would bring me joy and make me smile, because of this fear I had. I sacrificed trips because I thought, 'What if the plane crashes?' What if I drown in a swimming pool that's only four feet deep all the way around? I had all these irrational, bizarre thoughts. It gradually took my life away from me.

In what area have you allowed the hard knocks in this life to steal your happiness and fulfillment away from you? I know sometimes the task that lies ahead of you can seem daunting. Your circumstance is like a mountain in front of you and you may feel as if there is nothing to hope for. This is where I want to encourage you today. I want you to know that your life is not over. Where you stand may feel lonely. You may feel as if you're walking this road all by yourself. It may feel like no one in the world understands you. But I want you to know that you are not alone. There are millions of people all over the world who feel exactly what you are feeling in this very moment.

Although it won't change your circumstance, it is somehow encouraging to know that there's nothing wrong with you. There are thousands and maybe even millions of people currently facing the same struggle as you. You are not the problem. Find comfort in knowing that every human being on the planet struggles at one time or another. We don't face the same battles, but everyone struggles. Regardless of where you find yourself on the spectrum of struggles, know that your struggle still matters. You may never have known the feeling of extreme hunger or the abject fear of not having enough food to feed your family. Maybe that's not your path, but that doesn't mean that your path and your struggles are any less relevant than anyone else's.

The first step in your journey to taking back control of the wheel of your life is realizing and understanding that struggles are part of the journey. Even though you can't see it at the time, struggles almost always lead to the strength you need to go on.

I recall being in Jamaica on my honeymoon. One of the most awe-inspiring things we were able to witness there was the birth of sea turtles. If you do not know much about sea turtles, they are an endangered species. Because of this it's very rare to be at the right place and time to observe what we were about to see.

On the day the sea turtles were getting ready to hatch and head to the ocean, all the guests were brought to the beach in order to witness this event. As we were standing there, the sea turtles began to hatch; they began fighting, clawing, and crawling out of their eggs. It was amazing because as soon as they came out, they instinctively started heading straight to the ocean.

The national guide warned us not to touch the turtles under any circumstance. He gave no explanation why, though. Finally, a few of the turtles came out of the eggs right near our feet. Several of them exited their eggs on their backs. They were struggling to right themselves, fighting for their lives. You could see their little legs giving everything they had to flip over so that they could crawl to their destination.

A lady standing close to us couldn't take it anymore. She wasn't going to allow this turtle to continue to struggle. She reached down to flip it over. The guide happened to see her. With everything inside of him, he yelled at her to stop. She was startled and asked why she couldn't help the tiny turtle. The guide said, "What you don't realize is that the strength the turtle needs to survive in the ocean is built during the fight to the water."

You need to realize that your struggles, much like that turtle, are giving you the strength that you need to propel you to the next level in your life. Maybe you have a goal or dream or even a place that you feel in your heart you're supposed to be at. But because of the struggles and adversity life has brought your way, there's a disconnect between that dream and your reality. I'm here to encourage you that these difficulties are what is building the strength that you need to make it to your ultimate destination.

If you're struggling right now, I want to embolden you to not give up on your goals. Understand that it's okay not to be okay. Realize that everything you've ever gone through in life, every time things haven't gone your way, every time you've loved and lost, every single time you've found yourself in an adverse situation, you've made it to the other side. Because you're still standing. And not only are you still standing, you're still moving forward as you're reading this book.

Life is hard, but your life is not over. As long as warm blood still runs through your veins and there's breath in your lungs, you're still here. As long as you get up every day, no matter how mundane or routine it may seem, purpose still exists in your life. There are things you can accomplish. There are things you *will* accomplish that you can't even fathom if you choose to not give up. Yes, life is hard, but you are stronger than you realize, and you have the ability to do great things in this world. It's time to dig in and fight back. Why? Because YOU CAN.

Vital Reflections to Discuss or Journal:

1. *What type of struggles or difficulties have you faced in life? What difficulties are you facing currently? Explain in detail.*

2. *Have you ever wished you could erase any of those challenges?*

3. *How does it make you feel to know that you aren't alone in your struggles?*

4. *How does knowing that your struggles will eventually lead to strength encourage and comfort you in this moment?*

Chapter 3

THE IMAGINARY STANDARD

From birth, you were destined to be great. Literally from the moment you entered this earth, you were filled with life, purpose, and passion. Your passion at that time was milk and how to find it expeditiously, but nevertheless, you still had passion for something and were filled with life. You had a twinkle in your eyes, and your parents knew, those around you knew, and everyone who saw you knew that you were going to be special. You were going to be a world changer. You were going to be someone who left their mark on this earth and made it a better place.

You were born unique and special. You were born into this world for a very specific purpose to do something that only you can do. No one else can do it. There is no one else in the entire world with the exact same makeup and DNA as you, and that's a fact to marvel at in itself.

From the time you were a small child, you were nurtured and cared for and you believed anything was possible. At some point, early in your life, if you rewind your memory back long enough, you will recall a time in your life where you believed that everything was possible. You believed that you could go and change the world. Maybe you believed you would be an astronaut, a doctor, a lawyer, a scientist, or even a professional athlete.

Because of this belief, you had dreams, goals, and passions. Most importantly, you had uniqueness. There's something about every single one of us that makes us more unique than any other. Maybe it's the high-pitched, squeaky sound or snort you make when you laugh. Perhaps it's the way your eyes squint or the way your cheeks close your eyes completely when you're excited and smiling. It could be the way you move, or walk, or even the way you speak. Whatever it is, you are unique. You have characteristics that separate you from everyone else in the world.

As you began your own personal journey called life, you found yourself in foreign places like schools. If you're like me, some of your earliest memories revolve around elementary school classrooms. This is one of the first times you learned just how cruel the world can be. For as long as you can remember, your parents told you nothing but how great you were. Then you step into a foreign environment with 25 other children whose parents all told them the same thing.

Everyone's background is different, with different nurturing and support systems. Because of this, it was the first time you ran into bullies. You were playing with friends, just trying to connect. You were trying to thrive and survive in a foreign environment as a small child, and you happened to express your uniqueness in a place you thought was safe. Maybe you laughed and snorted, and all the other children began to point at you and laugh. All of us can identify with this moment of feeling like the oddball. Feeling out of place. That you don't belong in that moment. Feeling hurt, as if you're not enough.

What do you think you did when you saw all those fingers pointing and laughing? I'll tell you what you did. You became a little less you. You decided it hurts too badly to be ridiculed and mocked for something that makes you unique, so you began to step outside of who you were originally created to be. You became a little less you.

You then cautiously moved throughout your elementary school years. You had a few friends and it wasn't so bad. Until you reached middle school and that ever-so awkward age when things were changing – hormones, bodies, voices. It was a cesspool of disaster waiting to happen. You found yourself in a place where you slipped again. You expressed another piece of your uniqueness. Maybe it was the way you ran or how you pronounced a certain word, but it happened again. You became the center of attention for all the wrong reasons. Everyone was pointing and laughing and belittling you, and you became a little less you again.

In high school, the same thing happened. This process repeated itself throughout all the years of your life from the time you were a small child until you graduated. It happened so many times. You molded and shaped your life so much that you don't even recognize the person that you look at when you look in a mirror. When you connect with friends and hang out, you don't even recognize the person you've become because you've shapeshifted so many times in order to be accepted.

It doesn't end there, either. Once you fast forward, you find yourself in adulthood, whether it's on a college campus or in the workforce. All you want, what everyone wants, is to be successful and to find a place where you belong. I know that every single one of you reading this knows the feeling all too well of wanting to find a place where you're accepted. Every human being in existence longs for three very basic fundamental things: to be genuinely loved, deeply cared for, and accepted for who you truly are.

You want to be loved by those you care about, your family, a significant other, and your children. You want to be deeply cared for and to know that you matter. You want to know that people genuinely care when you go through things. When you hurt, you want to know that someone understands. And you want to be accepted for who you truly are. You long to be accepted for all that uniqueness and expression that makes you distinctly who you are.

There's nothing wrong with these feelings, but herein lies the dilemma we face with those genuine desires. The deadly assassin known as comparison creeps into your heart and causes you to sabotage yourself. Comparison threatens your desires for love, care, and acceptance. You retreat even further away from the emotional security you desperately desire.

You're surrounded by friends who are always taking their dream vacations. They're going all over the world every year. They're in Paris for two weeks and you only have one week of vacation for the entire year. Yet, here they are spending two weeks abroad at a time. Then they take a quick weekend trip to Vegas, posting selfies of themselves going to concerts and doing all the things you wish you could be doing.

Perhaps you and your spouse or significant other have been longing for a date night. It's been months since you've been out because your life revolves around the kids. Or it could be there's not enough cash flow to even be able to have a date night. You want to spend some time with that person you love so dearly. You open up Facebook, Instagram, or Twitter, and there it is. You see your friends having a date night. They're having a romantic night out with an incredible meal at an amazing restaurant.

You continue to scroll. You think that you're not going to let it bother you. Only then you see another friend who's just bought their dream home, their forever home, and you're still living in your very first starter home you moved into right out of college. You start to feel something inside of you begin to slowly crawl up, creep into a corner and die. You begin to feel less. You begin to feel not good enough, as if what they have is better than what you have.

Comparison is a dangerous titan of an adversary because it largely exists within our own minds. It manipulates you into falling for one of the greatest traps that is slowly and consistently taking our lives away from us. It's killing us a little bit every single day. No one sets out to compare their lives to someone else. In fact, you know you shouldn't, but it doesn't stop you from doing it anyway. You need to know that no one's existence is less than or greater than anyone else's.

You're looking at your friends on social media, and guess what? You only see their successes. No one is posting their greatest adversities online. They may post something at the end of their adversity, once they've overcome and are the hero of their story. Then we see it. Very few individuals are posting while they're in the middle of the crisis. We don't see them sitting on the side of the road with a flat tire. They don't want you to see that. They're only posting afterwards when the crisis has been averted. There are a few who are the exception, but the majority of people are not being transparent and open.

When you look at social media, you're seeing a person's highlight reel. They have to get the perfect angle and filter in order to get the perfect picture, the perfect family photo. It's all a façade. There is no such thing as a perfect family, a perfect job, or a perfect life. Nothing in this world is perfect. The sooner you accept that, the sooner you can appreciate the life that you have. You will never be able to love the life you live until you begin to realize that your life is special. You have to learn to appreciate and focus on what you already have and stop focusing so much on what you don't have. When you begin to notice what you do have, you'll recognize that you have a lot more than you think.

The problem, though, is there is this imaginary standard in society that says if you aren't at a certain level of accomplishment by a certain time in your life, then you are not successful. That's what society says, and too many of us measure ourselves according to this made-up standard. Nobody's life is literally being judged.

Look at Colonel Sanders from KFC. After much turmoil in his early life, he created his award-winning recipe for chicken and became a millionaire in his 60s. He got divorced and nearly lost everything he had, but then he built his fortune in the latter years of his life. No one is going to look at Colonel Sanders and say that guy was unsuccessful because he didn't have a dream family or a perfect job where he made his millions and retired at 60. The bulk of his legacy started at 60.

If that's the case, you need to realize that this standard you're trying to live up to doesn't really exist. Society says you have to be here by this time, which is a lie. As you're reading this, maybe you find yourself having felt this pressure. Maybe you felt like you should have graduated college in four years instead of the seven it actually took you. Perhaps you feel like you should have gotten your dream job and purchased your first home as soon as you graduated, but instead you're working odd jobs just to make ends meet. You haven't found a career yet because the job market is so difficult right now.

You're trying to figure out why that close friend of yours came right out of college and landed their dream job. It seems as if everything is perfect. But you don't know that they have their own monsters they're facing. You don't know whether a close relative might have decided to pay for their school and help them land that job. But in return, they have to give so much back just to make it up or they're indebted to this person forever. How could you realize whether they have to live with that hanging over their head?

You don't know what other people went through to get where they are, or what they're still dealing with as a result. I could name countless instances of celebrities who seemed to have it all, and without a moment's notice they took their own lives. That person that you're so desperately comparing your life to, wishing you had what they had, is no longer in existence because they were unhappy also.

You need to stop trying to live up to this standard that is shaping your life, because the gap between this imaginary standard and your present reality is called frustration. If there was a big goal you wanted to accomplish by a certain time and it's taking you a little longer than you thought it would take you, you now find yourself frustrated. You start to feel that you're inadequate or less than. You're downtrodden. You start to question your purpose. You are falling asleep at the wheel of your life. The frustration continues to mount up steadily. It breaks you down and kills your drive. It makes you wonder, 'What's the point of even pressing on?'

You know there are people in your life who love you and depend on you. It's almost as if it doesn't matter, though, because from the time you were a small child you've been focusing on shifting and shaping your life. You've done this all the way into adulthood. You continue to try to keep up with the Joneses and impress people who don't really love or care about you. You're feeling empty all the while, but still posting those wonderful selfies on social media so that the world can think you are enough.

I have news for you. You have to stop living by this standard, and you have to stop worrying about what the world thinks. That part of you when you were a small child who believed anything was possible... that is who you are. You are that person with the unique laugh or smile, that person with the unique walk or run. And you're that person with that unique birthmark or beauty mark on your face. No matter what it is, that is who you are, and who you are is more than enough!

You are more than enough. I want you to repeat this. I want you to say this out loud: I am more than enough. It's time for you to stop looking for the world to affirm your humanity, your greatness, and your gifts and start practicing your own daily affirmations. One of the greatest things I've learned in my journey was to tell myself that I am great, I am strong, I am courageous, and I am enough. Those are things I say to myself every day. Yours don't have to be the same as mine, but you do have to speak positively to yourself.

Negative self-talk is one of the leading killers of drive, motivation, and passion in this life. It's something you do when you feel like you are not enough. Maybe the negative self-talk you practice is because you were taught that behavior. It's a learned response because somebody close to you tore you down instead. Someone you thought would nurture and love you told you that you weren't enough, and you accepted their thoughts and began to repeat those things to yourself.

Every time you make a mistake in life, you don't give yourself grace. You will allow everyone else around you to make mistakes and freely give them grace. If your best friend forgets something, it's okay. If your spouse messes up, it's okay. If your children make a mistake, it's okay. But when it comes to you, you beat yourself up. You say you're not enough.

You do this so much that you begin to feel like throwing in the towel. You've drifted off at the wheel of your life and instead of living your life to the fullest, instead you're walking dead. You're showing up to functions, gatherings, or meetings and you're a shell of your former self. All the while, you're looking at the people around you. You see how beautiful they are, how well adorned they look in their clothes, and are trying to figure out how you can become more like them.

It's time for you to stop trying to become more like anyone except for yourself. The greatest gift that you have to offer this world is to be 100 percent uniquely you. You were created and handcrafted by the Almighty to be who you are. Not to be your friend, your cousin, your co-worker, or some random stranger you see on the internet who only shows you their beauty without exposing their struggles. You weren't created to be them. They were created to be them. Everyone has their own mission. They have their own circumstances they have to overcome, their own monsters and internal demons they have to face. They have their own success plan and path.

You have your own path. Your path is no less than or more than anyone else's. But it's your path. It's a beautiful path filled with pain and pleasure, grief and joy, love and amazing, never-ending opportunities. Even if you've had a lot of negative moments up to this point and you're waiting on your time to win because you see everyone else winning, just know that all it takes is one moment. Will you be ready for your moment? It's time for you to start focusing on giving yourself love and care. It's time to recognize the uniqueness that you are.

In the entire universe, there's not one single human being that is exactly like you. And that means you are pretty special. Once you realize you are special, no matter what anyone else thinks, no matter how anyone else's life is going, you'll realize that your life matters. Your life is powerful. Your existence is needed, and your purpose is in front of you. It's time for you to take back the wheel of your life. Because YOU CAN.

Vital Reflections to Discuss or Journal:

1. *Have you ever fallen into the trap of comparing your life to someone else's? Why or why not?*

2. *Often times, you are your own worst enemy. Why do you put so much pressure on yourself to live up to the "imaginary standard" discussed in the chapter above?*

3. *In the entire universe, there's only one you. You are extremely unique and valuable. How do these facts make you feel?*

4. *What are a few ways you can begin to stop comparing yourself to others and start appreciating your own journey in life? Explain.*

Chapter 4

THE WAKEUP CALL

A few years ago, I was traveling on a trip for work and I had an opportunity to go to a conference that would help me grow and develop in many areas of my life. I was very excited about this because I love to travel. I've always loved new experiences and new places because it makes me feel alive. In this instance, I reached my destination and got all settled and nestled into my hotel room for the night. There's something about when you first arrive at a hotel, that clean room smell and fresh bedding. When you lie down, it just feels great. It's very easy for you to find yourself sleeping your time away, and many hotels understand this.

After checking into the hotel, I took my time getting settled into my room. Late that evening, the phone in my room began ringing. I couldn't imagine who was calling me so late. I answered and it was the front desk clerk. He said, "Hello, sir. I know you're here for the business conference and wanted to ask you a quick question. Would you like a wakeup call?"

This was a little puzzling at first. I thought, "A wakeup call? What is this? Am I in high school?" I say that jokingly, but in all seriousness, they asked that question for a very specific reason. People go to events all the time and miss them because they oversleep. They don't mean to oversleep. They don't plan to oversleep, but that bed is just so comfortable. It feels so great in the moment that they forget to set an alarm. Perhaps the alarm fails, or the phone decides to update overnight and resets itself.

Whatever the reason, the alarm doesn't go off when it's needed the most.

The front desk clerk went on to explain that the hotel had a system in place just in case I accidentally slept too long. He explained they would give me a call to ensure that I didn't miss out on the very purpose of why I was there. He said, "We'll make sure that you are awake and ready to go!"

Sometimes in life, my friend, we need a wakeup call. I remember when life brought me mine, and it was one of the scariest, most terrifying situations of my entire life. It happened in high school, but it didn't start off so scary. It started as a rather routine evening at church. Three of my best friends and I were getting ready to go to a Battle of the Bands competition with the youth group after church along with several of our peers. We had a 15-passenger van, and everyone loaded up in it.

A few younger kids ran up to the van right before we left and asked if they could come along as well. Our driver explained that unfortunately the van was full and there wasn't space for them. My friend didn't want anyone to miss out, so he said, "You know what? If kids want to go, we're old enough. I'll drive my car to make more room in the van." So my three friends and I hopped in his car and off we went.

We drove to Memphis, Tennessee where the Battle of the Bands was held. It was an incredible experience. We had so much fun laughing, clowning around, and having a blast doing what teenage boys do. As the evening came to a conclusion, we headed back to our vehicles. A small hilarious argument began to take place between myself and one of my friends. My friend called, "Shotgun! I'm sitting in the front seat."

I said to him, "No, I'm sitting in the front seat." He argued that I had sat in the front seat on the way there, to which I responded, "It doesn't matter. I'm bigger than you. End of discussion." The argument continued the entire walk back to the car. Eventually I stepped back and gave in, allowing him to take the front seat. We then took off and headed home.

It was a regular, routine drive as we made our way back. Not very long into our drive, my friend pulled over into a gas station. He didn't go to a gas pump, and he didn't get out to go inside to purchase anything. This was a little puzzling to me, so I asked him if everything was okay. He responded, "Yeah, you okay?" After assuring him I was fine, we still sat there for a few more minutes.

Before we could leave, the friend who I had been arguing with over the front seat changed his mind and offered to let me have the coveted front seat. "Seriously," I said, "I'm already in the car, man. I'm situated." He insisted, though, and got out of the car. I followed his lead and we traded seats. There was no reason for this, but we did it anyways. Once we were back inside, we left the gas station and headed down the interstate.

We drove for about 15 minutes and were about halfway home when the unexpected happened. I remember it like it was yesterday, and I can still hear and feel the moment to this day. I was half asleep when I heard one of the loudest explosions I've ever heard in my life. Startled, my eyes flew open and I asked what happened. My friend driving the car frantically said he didn't know what happened, and as the words left his mouth, the car began to shake violently and jump up and down. In the next instant, the car began fishtailing.

By now, everyone in the car was yelling, and then it happened. The car flew off the interstate at 75 miles per hour. It barreled into a steep ditch off the side of the highway, spinning out in the air, knocking down tree after tree after tree. I can remember hearing the sound of glass shattering into millions of pieces and seeing it fly by as we continued flying deeper into the ditch. It was flying everywhere, hitting me in the face. My head was slapping back and forth against the car seat and the window. And finally, booooooom! We hit a tree so hard that the car immediately came to an abrupt stop, completely accordioned and smashed in.

In that instant, my eyes were closed, and fear overtook my entire body. All I could think about was what I thought to be the inevitable, that my greatest fear in this life had come to pass and this was the end of my journey here on earth. I also couldn't help remembering one of my closest friends and football teammates who had passed away in a car accident just over a year before. He was killed in a sudden accident on the back roads of our small town, Hernando, MS. He and another friend were driving half the speed we were, but they lost control of the car and my good friend crashed into a tree, was pinned behind the wheel, and lost his life in the process. And I thought, this is the end for me, as well.

God had other plans that day. I finally opened my eyes and my body was still intact. I slowly checked in with each of my friends, DJ, Justin, and Tony. All of us appeared to be okay, other than one friend who was hyperventilating and having a hard time catching his breath initially. As we all began to frantically look around at one another to try to figure out what to do next, smoke began billowing out of the car. Maybe we had watched too many movies, but we thought the car was going to explode - with us inside. We all tried to open the doors to get out, but they were pinned shut because the metal of the car was accordioned so deeply. It was impossible to get out.

You hear stories about people who have superhuman strength in an emergency, and that's what happened here. I know exactly where my strength came from at that moment too. It wasn't me and it wasn't adrenaline. I am thankful that the Creator, my God, gave me the strength to push the door entirely off of the hinges, creating a small opening barely big enough for all of us to crawl out of the car and make our way back toward the road.

This evening ended with four young men walking away from an accident that should have taken every single one of our lives and ended them that moment, leaving our family, friends, and loved ones in a wake of grief like so many others have unfortunately had to experience. But that is not how the story ended. We all stood up. There was a doctor who had just gotten off shift from a nearby hospital and was driving home when he saw the accident. Before we even made it out of the ditch, he had already called 911. He checked us out at the scene before the ambulances could even arrive.

As this happened, I couldn't help but think, why am I still here? This led me on a journey over the course of the next few years through college. I was trying to figure out my way and my path. I couldn't come to terms with the question of, why am I here when my friend is not? I never got an answer to that question, but this is where I landed. God kept me here on this planet for a reason, and since He did, I will devote the remainder of my life trying to figure out the path and the purpose for which I was created. I will continue to search for why He spared my life on that cool fall night.

This wasn't an easy process or an easy journey for me to go on. I found myself struggling in every area of my life. I began questioning my faith, wondering what the point was. Wondering what my purpose was and how to find my place in God's Kingdom. I was having issues with my family, arguing and butting heads with my parents. I was staying away from the house more and more; when I was there, I was mistreating my siblings.

Life was one big struggle. I started having financial problems because of overspending. I was spending every penny I had buying clothes and other flashy things to impress people that I no longer interact with today. I also struggled with my fitness. I had always been in shape and taken care of myself. I played football, baseball, basketball, track, and all the sports. Name the sport and I played it. Sports had always been a huge part of my life. But for the first time in my life, I was eating myself into oblivion because I was so unhappy. I was so unfulfilled and desperately trying to find out, why am I here? Although I didn't understand it at the time, this was my wakeup call.

Perhaps as you read this, you can see yourself in this story. You see your own situation and circumstances. Maybe your story wasn't as extreme as a near-death experience in a wreck, but it was something else. Maybe your story was filled with abuse or neglect. It may not have even been neglect due to a lack of resources or poverty. Sometimes neglect stems from an abundance of resources. Perhaps your family had so much money that your parents were always working to keep up their standard of living.

Or possibly they were going to country clubs or traveling, and you were left alone with your tutors or your nanny.

No matter what your story was or what your struggles were, you may find yourself still having a hard time. As you're reading this, it hurts. Maybe you see yourself when you look at me, a lost young man trying desperately to find his way, wandering aimlessly through life, and questioning the very God who gave him life. It may be that you're questioning everything, questioning why.

Have you been slowly drifting? Have your eyes been getting heavy from carrying the weight of the world and making you so tired to the point where you're just going? You feel like you're wandering aimlessly. It seems like you're not working towards anything or accomplishing anything along the way. You think that everybody has it better than you, and you are simply existing through life as it passes you by day after day.

It could be that it's even worse than that. It could be that you're like I was in the first chapter. You find yourself completely asleep at the wheel of your life. You no longer feel anything and are numb to all of the emotions that life brings. You gave your best effort. You tried desperately and gave everything you had into building a life, and you still find yourself completely asleep at the wheel. Or perhaps you don't even realize you're asleep. I am here to tell you that every single part of my journey including the accident was part of my story. And it was relevant because it led me to this very moment.

My question to you is, do you want something different? Are you tired of going through the motions? Are you tired of settling for less than what you truly deserve? If the answer to any of these questions is yes, this is your wakeup call. My passion and my purpose is simply this: I want to help you truly live and not simply be alive. Not only that, I want you to love the life that you live. With all of the passion, energy, and fervor inside of me I believe that you can live life and love it, and I have a foundation that I plan to unveil in this book where I will help you lay out the plan to take back control of the wheel of your life.

What I learned through the entire process is that, yes, struggles are a part of life, and you cannot control getting to the point where you're falling asleep. But now I'm going to make sure that you don't miss out, just like that courtesy clerk at that hotel who made sure that I would not miss out on the very reason why I was there. You were created to do and accomplish great and incredible things, and I'm going to ensure that you don't miss out on a single thing. I want to make sure that you feel passion, love, and life again and that you recognize that blessings exist all around you.

So many times, you go outside and you're driving down the street. The sky is bright blue, and the sun is shining. There's a cool breeze blowing, and you have everything you need to make it through the day. Yet there's some instance, something negative that's hanging over your head. Maybe somebody cut you off on the way to work; now your entire day is thrown off because you're so upset. Perhaps you received bad news as you were walking out the door and it overshadows everything positive that you have, all the things that you love.

You end up losing perspective. Your small children require all of the energy and effort in the world. They're tiring. Yes you, mom, give everything you have trying to feel like you're enough while fighting not to compare yourself to others. But you end up feeling "mom guilt" for doing what you thought was best for your child. While you're so busy worrying about what other people might think of you as a mom, you lose sight that the precious life you helped create is right in front of you. You forget that your children are the greatest gift ever given to you.

You often take for granted the simple blessings you have because you're looking instead for those big answers in life. All the while, you're taking for granted the things that you have. It is time to stop focusing on what you do not have. As long as you focus on what you don't have, you will never have enough. You will never feel satisfied, fulfilled, or happy. You will never experience true joy that sustains you through life. Instead, all you'll be left with is a feeling of inadequacy, of not having enough or being enough.

If you really want things to change, it's time for you to start taking stock. When was the last time you made a list of everything you are thankful for? It will blow your mind if you take time to think about and process everything that you do have. One of the most incredible ways to stay positive is to constantly practice an attitude of gratitude.

Gratitude is what helps keep everything in perspective. It helps you keep your mind set on the right things. It keeps you afloat and helps you stay hopeful, looking forward to what could be rather than what isn't. You often focus on what you lack, when in reality you're not lacking at all. Even if you are lacking in some areas, chances are you more than make up for it in other areas.

So, this is it, my friend. It's time for you to wake up once and for all. What are you thankful for? What do you have? I'm here to tell you that you have everything because you have life and you have a tomorrow. As long as you have a tomorrow, your yesterdays are history, but tomorrow is greatness. Everything you ever wanted lies in front of you, and it's time for us to journey together to go get it. Let's make it happen together. Because WE CAN!

Vital Reflections to Discuss or Journal:

1. *The purpose of the wakeup call is to capture your attention to help you regain focus. Do you have an experience like the one above that changed your life forever? If so, please share.*

2. *In what area(s) of your life do you currently need a wakeup call?*

3. *Do you have a system in place to practice gratitude daily? If not, how can you start one today?*

4. *Are you ready to wake up and seize control of your life? It's time to dream again! What are 5 major things you want to accomplish before the end of your life?*

Chapter 5

FACING YOUR GIANTS

You've heard my story, and it was one filled with all types of drama, chaos, adversity, and even near death. But this isn't about me right now. This is your wakeup call. The question that's currently on the table is, what is your story? Your story may not be as extreme as mine. Your story may be more extreme than mine. It doesn't really matter. Often when I've told my story to people and asked them to share theirs in return, they say things like, "My life hasn't been nearly as exciting as that," or "My life has mostly been sadness," or even, "My story is so anticlimactic compared to your story."

Saying things like this is something you need to stop doing. It's another form of negative self-talk. Never downplay the significance of your journey. Every human being on the planet has their own journey in which they walk. They have their own epic destiny they're in the process of living out. And that applies to you, as well. You are now currently in the process of living out your epic journey.

When your story is told at the end of your days, it will be so beautiful you won't even be able to fathom it. No matter how ugly some parts of the story were, how difficult some of the chapters were, or how extremely hopeless you may have felt at times, your story will end beautifully. But right now, you must discover what your story is. So often you don't take the time to reflect back over your life and look at those things which made you who you are today. You will never know where you're going unless you know where you've been. Until you begin to look through and evaluate your life, you won't be able to become all that you can. You won't be able to build a life that you love to live.

Building this new foundation in your life begins by realizing that your story is powerful. Your life story is one that is beautiful, one that deserves to be told, and one that matters. You matter. Your story matters: your heart, your struggles and triumphs, your sadness and joy. It all matters.

You must never compare your story to someone else's story, because every one of our stories are different. That difference is why we enjoy great stories. The beauty in this world is the diversity that we share. If every human being and every story were the same, it would be boring. Nothing would stand out. There would be none of the colorful things that we get to enjoy in this beautiful world.

Once you recognize the uniqueness of you and your story and begin to reflect back over your life, you're going to come to some of those points in your life that were not so happy. You'll remember those parts of life that you like to overlook, that make you sad to think about. You'll even recall things that leave a heavy feeling in the pit of your stomach as you begin to think about your childhood and what you endured. Perhaps it was the abuse you faced or the neglect you experienced. It could be the learning disability you had to work through or the bullying you faced because of it. Whatever it is, as you begin to reflect over your story, it takes you back to a time in your life where you felt as if you weren't enough.

You need to understand that you are not defined by your experiences in this life. When you think back through some of your experiences you may feel ashamed. You are not what happened to you. As a matter of fact, you are more than what has happened to you. You are greatness. You were created with purpose and passion.

Unfortunately, we live in a world where there are manipulators and people looking to harm others. Evil exists around us and feeds on the hearts and minds of the innocent, and maybe you remember having your innocence taken away from your far too soon by something that was completely out of your control. When you think back on those times it's disheartening and makes you feel heavy.

Everyone faced different things in their childhood. For you, maybe it was the playground bully who talked about you and belittled you. Maybe you were beat down because even though your parents were working as hard as they could, they still couldn't afford the name-brand clothes. You didn't have the nicest jacket. Maybe you had to wear your older sibling's jacket that was handed down to you because your parents were doing all they could just to put food on the table and pay the bills.

Children can be so cruel at times. Although it may be unintentional, it still drives home certain points that are hammered into your heart. It's hammered into you that you were less than because of what you didn't have. It's hammered into you that you were not good enough, that you didn't belong, that you didn't fit in, that there's no place for you. Then perhaps you went home, and your parents had a toxic relationship that consisted of arguments and fighting.

Or it could be instead that your parents weren't present at all. Maybe your dad was always busy traveling for work and all you wanted was to have a relationship with him. And that left your mom home alone to take care of everything. Maybe she was always tired from dragging you and your siblings from one event to another, checking homework, washing clothes, and making dinner, and at the end of the day she just kind of checked out. All you wanted was for someone to hear you and tell you that you matter, but she wasn't present.

Perhaps this then led you down a path in your life of shame, doubt, guilt, and frustration. Maybe you were left feeling helpless, as though everything was taken from you and you didn't deserve to be loved. Feeling as if you can never open your heart again. Feeling empty. Walking this road can leave you feeling unfulfilled and unhappy. When you revisit these days, you're often left with a feeling of hopelessness.

Maybe you find yourself in one or more of the scenarios I just mentioned. The reality is all of us have gone through something. Nobody's life is completely perfect and beautiful all the time. No matter how much social media might say otherwise, this simply is not the case. If you want to step up and realize there's more to life, it begins with you acknowledging that you are more. More than what you've been through.

Everything that you've gone through in this life was simply a season of preparation for greater things to come in your future. The greater the adversity in this life, the stronger you become.

Strength is built in the struggle. Your strength, your passion, everything you are is built through the fires that you face in life.

When I was a kid, I often fell victim to the mentality of why. I often wondered why me. Why did I have to go through so many hurtful situations? I was bullied as a kid throughout school. We didn't have a lot of money, so I didn't have the greatest clothes. I had a lot of family who cared for me deeply and would buy me things for the holidays, but I was also a growing boy who grew very fast and grew out of things quickly. Because of this, I usually ended up shopping at Walmart for my clothes. The other children were cruel and made a mockery of me; they laughed at me and belittled me.

There were also people throughout my life who made comments to me. Sometimes it was a teacher. Sometimes it was a close relative. Sometimes it was even a friend. They would say things like, "You're not smart," or "You won't ever be anything in this life." Other times I heard comments like, "You'll never be successful because you're lazy," and even, "You're a failure."

There were all these labels that were imposed upon me, and I'm sure you know exactly what that feels like because there were labels imposed upon you, as well. There have been things that you've been called and things you've been told that you've worn as if they were a brand on your very skin all throughout your life to this very day. No matter what age you are, you've worn some of those labels so much so that it has affected every area of your life.

These labels have affected your family and your ability to love your spouse or partner well. They've affected your ability to love your children. You're not able to open up to them and let them feel warmth because of your own insecurity. You're not able to nurture your own children because you've been told you weren't good enough. You shield yourself from the love that the people around you want so desperately to give because you believe you're not worthy of love.

Those are all lies, and in order to become who you are meant to become you have to realize this, identify the lies in your own life, and kick them out of your head once and for all. You have to face your giants. You are strong. You're a warrior, and there is a hero dwelling deep down inside of you. In order to activate that hero, you have to face your giants.

In my life I've had to face one giant after another. I wish we lived in a world where everything was perfect and beautiful. Where there was no evil or hatred and things of this nature didn't exist. But the sad reality is that I've been mistreated. As an African American male, there have been times I've been criticized, ostracized, and even discriminated against because of the color of my skin.

I have been belittled time and time again. I've had multiple figures in my life tell me that I wasn't enough, tell me what I did not have, or tell me what I would not become. They have said and done things to intentionally cause me to fail. And in order to become who I was meant to be, I had to come face to face with all of those words. I had to look at myself in the mirror and rehear those voices saying all of those nasty, hurtful things. I had to look myself directly in my eyes and relive everything.

No matter how boldly I smiled to pretend as if the words did not affect me, the reality is those words buried themselves deep within my heart. It wasn't until I made a choice to come face to face with myself in the mirror that things began to change. I began to take out all of those words that were said about me and write them down. When I did this, it was as if I was reaching into my heart. I started pulling out those messages that were so neatly tucked away in my heart. I unfolded them and began to label them as the lies that they are: I am not a failure or a mistake, I am not lazy, I am not worthless, and I am not less than. I then replaced those lies with truths. I am bold. I am courageous and brave. I am an overcomer.

What giants do you have in your life? Until you face them, you're never going to become who you want to be. You're never going to wake up and take back control of the wheel of your life as long as you allow the voices of the past to haunt your future, your forever. As long as you allow those childhood bullies who told you that you weren't enough to be your dictators you'll never become the strong, courageous warrior you are meant to be. Unless you think back and come to terms with the lies of even your parents, that teacher, that coach, or friend, you'll never be able to move forward. Until you come face to face with your giant and realize that yes, you can accomplish anything you put your mind to, you will never become who you're meant to be.

I'm here to tell you that you can become exactly who you want to be in this world, and this is how you do it. You have to face those monsters that exist to take life away from you, those monsters that have been haunting you from your childhood and are still haunting you today. Worry, anxiety, and depression are running rampant and taking your life from you. They're killing you, going back to that standard that you're trying to live up to. You haven't come face to face with the root cause of what is killing you to begin with. It's easier to live life at the surface level where it's safe, so you live in the symptom rather than the root cause of your problems.

I wasn't able to move forward until I came to grips with my own monster of anxiety. It still haunts me to this day, but not like it once did. I can't stop anxiety from coming and knocking on my door. I can't stop that monster from coming to visit when it's time for me to go to bed and my mind should be at peace. But what I can do is stand up and fight. I can say, "You've taken control and taken me captive in my own life for far too long, but I refuse to let you do so anymore!"

That is a proclamation I want you to make in this very moment. If you have an opportunity, look in a mirror while you do this. Regardless, I want you to pause what you're doing and really say these words and let them register in your heart. I want you to name your monster. I want you to name that thing that's been haunting you. That thing that's been keeping you from living your best life. That thing that's holding you back from living the life of passion and purpose that you so desperately long for.

You have to stand up to that bully that has been taking your life from you for far too long. Whatever it is, I want you to say to it, "I no longer allow you to have control of my life!" I want you to say these words out loud: "You cannot control me or dictate my life anymore. You have no power over me. From this day forward, I will control my own life."

By doing this, you have resolved in your heart that power lives inside of you. You are more than an overcomer. Whatever has haunted you for far too long will not hold you captive anymore. Once you've come to the place where you have faced your monster, you are officially on the road to healing. Healing begins with accepting that which you cannot control. Facing your monsters means looking eye to eye with your deepest, darkest secrets and facing up to the things that drive you crazy and cause you anxiety. It's realizing that it is what it is.

I know it might sound cliché, but I cannot control any other human being on this planet. I couldn't control the people who mistreated me, the kids who spit at me, kicked me, or pushed me down. I couldn't change the kids who thought it was fun to laugh at me because of my clothes or because I was given hand-me-down shoes that were three sizes too big and flopped on my feet as I walked. My parents made just a little too much money for me to get free school lunches, but there were some days I didn't have enough money for lunch. I couldn't stop the kids who belittled me when this happened and thought it was funny to say, "Ha! You're so poor!"

As I've grown older, I cannot control when anxiety decides to present itself and tries to capture my breath and take my life away from me. I cannot control those things. You know what I can control, though? I can control myself. And you can control you. It's time for you to stop giving power to things, people, and circumstances that don't deserve power over you.

So many times, you show up to work and you feel miserable. You hate it because you have loud or hateful coworkers who snicker and laugh at you, or maybe even a rude boss. You allow things outside of your control to make you feel less than, worthless, or like you're not enough. It's time for you to accept the fact that you can't control them. You can only control your own response. And in your response, you have to resolve deep down in your heart that no other human being should be powerful enough to dictate how you move about your daily life, regardless of who they are or how close they are to you.

This next part may hit close to home for some of you. I completely understand submission to a spouse in a loving, warm, healthy relationship. But if you're in an abusive or toxic relationship that is unhealthy, you cannot allow another person's evil or hatred to soak into your heart so that you begin to respond the same way. You have to keep yourself free and pure from that because all you will do is drag yourself deep down into a hole.

You have to stop allowing things that are beyond your control make you react outside your character. This only weighs you down and makes you feel heavy, like you cannot go on any longer. It sometimes even brings you to a point where you contemplate the thought of not living anymore because of the words of another human being who is no more powerful, special, or worthy than yourself.

Their words cannot outweigh the words in your heart unless you allow them to. And you, my friend, are enough! You are more than enough. You are strong. You are a warrior. You are a phenomenal human being on the path to purpose and fulfillment.

It's time for us to free that hero living deep within you. Now that you have made a conscious choice to face your giants and to no longer allow them to control your actions and how you feel about life, healing can officially begin. It's time for you to face your giants, overcome them, and use them as a stepping stool to the next level in life. Why, you ask? Because you can.

Vital Reflections to Discuss or Journal:

1. *Do you ever downplay the significance of your own story? Why?*

2. *How can you begin to appreciate the uniqueness of your life story?*

3. *What are the giants in your own life that have haunted you and caused you not to live your best life?*

4. *You can't win a battle you're not willing to fight. Are you ready to dig deep and face your giants?*

5. *What specific strategies will you put into place to help you slay your giants once and for all?*

Chapter 6

UNLEASHING THE
SUPERHERO WITHIN

Everybody loves a good story. We all enjoy stories in different forms. You might enjoy the beauty of a book. To some, there's something about holding a physical book in your hands, feeling the pages turn, and taking in that nice, clean book smell as the wind hits your face. You're able to fully immerse yourself in the story as you read every little detail of a character, fully imagining what you might see.

Maybe you enjoy movies because you're a visual learner. You like to see things unfold, and sometimes you even take your imagination a step further. You try to explore in your mind what could have happened after the story on the screen is over. Perhaps instead you like listening to people tell stories and prefer audio books. Regardless of the method, every person loves a good story.

The thing that is so significant about good stories is that section in the middle that we all love to hate. You know what I'm talking about. You're watching a story and your favorite characters have faced some adversities, some stumbling blocks along the way. But even though they've hit a snag or two in life, they've managed to figure it out. Everything is going perfectly. Their relationship is going smoothly, and their job is going splendidly. Everything couldn't be more picture perfect if you had created it in your own mind.

And then it happens. When everything seems to be a little too good to be true, you start to get an uneasy feeling. You don't know how it's coming or in what form, but you know it's coming all the same, and when it hits you feel it. The plotline takes a twist and a turn, and your favorite character begins to experience real life-changing adversity, real sickness, real hurt, or real pain. All that beautiful, picturesque setup that happened before no longer matters now because it's all gone down the drain.

But that's the part of the story that makes it worth reading to begin with, because the story doesn't end there. The story continues, and that character has to come face-to-face with their own monsters like we discussed in the last chapter. When this happens, they have a really important choice to make that comes down to a couple things. Are they going to throw in the towel and give up on everything they've shared and tried so desperately to accomplish? Or are they going to stand up and fight for the life that they want?

In the best stories you read or watch, the character always rises to the occasion. They overcome adversity and go on to triumph in the end, often leaving you, if you're like myself, with a trail of tears and a warm heart. These stories captivate us because we love celebrating winners. We love rooting for the underdogs who go against all the odds to step up and overcome in order to move into the life they were created to live.

It's so ironic that we love these stories so much, especially the part when they overcome adversity. Because so many times when we face adversity in our own life, it's so easy to want to give up and throw in the towel. Maybe it's fear. Life can beat up on you. As we already discussed, life is hard, it doesn't play fair, and it takes no prisoners. I get all of that.

But knowing what we know about the most powerful stories, and knowing what we just discussed about how great adversity creates great strength, at what point in your life do you begin to ask yourself, why am I so afraid? Why am I so anxious? Why am I so ready to throw in the towel and give up on my own life?

When you're taking in a story, you're continually rooting and cheering the characters on. You're hoping they don't give up. You're even wishing that you could give personal advice about not giving up because you know it ends well. Guess what? Your life ends well, too. But you have to resolve in your heart that you won't give up when life comes swinging. You won't back down when life throws a haymaker out of left field and catches you completely off guard. You won't go down when you get that bad diagnosis from the doctor that you could never prepare yourself for, when all you can think about is the loved ones or friends that you've seen pass away from that very same diagnosis. It doesn't have to end for you there if you choose in your heart not to give up.

I know this from personal experience. A few years back, my wife and I had just found out we were pregnant with our second son. We couldn't have been more excited to know that we were getting to experience the miracle of life for a second time. That same week I had been suffering with a sinus infection. It was plaguing me and wouldn't go away. I'm all too familiar with sinus infections because my sinuses have always been a little off, and I get infections a couple times every year like clockwork.

I went to the doctor, explained I had a sinus infection and that I needed some medicine so I could get on with my life. Since I had never seen this particular doctor before, she wanted to check my vitals and do bloodwork to get a baseline for my health. I told her I understood that was important and that we should probably do that some other time. "I'm in a rush," I protested. I asked if she could just prescribe some medicine so I could be on my merry way.

The doctor was adamant, though, in wanting to check my vitals. She explained, "At your age and your weight, I really think it's important to check this." And as soon as she mentioned weight, I knew that ominous tone. That is something I always heard about and always wrestled with. I never struggled with drugs, alcohol, or any of a multitude of other things. I did, however, struggle with food, which was my drug of choice. From a young age, my weight had always been a battle and still is to this very day.

Once the doctor mentioned my weight, I gave in. I figured I should allow her to run her tests. She sent me to the lab for bloodwork, prescribed antibiotics for my sinus infection, and I left the office. The next day I received a call from the doctor. Frantically she said, "Sir, I hate to tell you this, but you need to come back and see me as soon as possible." Then came three words I didn't want to hear. "You have diabetes," she explained. My A1c levels were just into the diabetic range, but nevertheless, it was a diagnosis.

This hit me hard, because I've had family members who have died from diabetes. Diabetes is a terrible disease that some people have no control over because they're born with it, but others get it because of poor choices. Regardless, it's a terrible disease that kills so many. When I heard those words, all I could think about was the other news I had received that week. I had just found out about one of the most joyous things in my life. I was about to bring life to another beautiful baby boy, and all I could think was, "I may not even get to see him grow up."

The doctor prescribed several medications. She told me that if I didn't take them and stay on them continuously, I likely wouldn't live to the age of 40. I was only 30 years old at the time. No one can be prepared for a report like that, to hear that your life might end so early. That all of the things you love about this life – your family, your wife, your boys, all of the beauty that life brings you – may possibly be taken away. That you can take some pills to try to control it, but the side effects will probably make you feel sicker. Nobody is prepared to hear that. It's scary and shocking.

That's when you have to find the resolve that lies deep inside of you. Just like the choice of those characters in the story we discussed, you have to make a choice in your own life. Do you sink or swim? Do you run, or do you stand and fight? I'm happy to inform you that I stood, and I fought. I fought for my life. I had a reason to keep fighting, because I didn't want my wife to have to raise two boys on her own, to have to be both mommy and daddy. I didn't want my boys to have to grow up without a father to teach them the ways of the world and how to survive and thrive.

Once I found myself in this place, I fought, and I fought, and I fought some more. I didn't take any of the pills. I'm not telling you not to take your pills because we each must do what's best for us individually. Maybe I'm a little stubborn, but I did my research and just refused to be limited to one outcome. I decided I was going to find another way. I dug deep inside of me, and I found a new gym. I gained a fitness community. I built new, healthy habits. When I got all these things into place, I went hard. I did everything I could, and I fought for my life. And in a year's time, I was able to officially reverse the diagnosis of diabetes. The doctor was completely shocked by this because she knew I didn't take the medications. She told me that whatever I was doing, keep doing it.

Nobody can prepare you for all of the adversities that life will throw your way. No one can prepare you for having your dream job, the one that you've given everything to, fought for and sacrificed for, and then being informed out of the blue that they have to let you go. It's not based on your performance, because you've been an incredible employee, but due to finances they have to make cuts. No one is prepared to lose people that they love and are close to unexpectedly through tragedy, accidents, or murder. Nobody can be ready for life to hit you that way.

That is where you find yourself today. You find yourself in a fight, where you're that character in your own story that we discussed. You're at the point where you have to ask yourself, do I give up or stay strong? Do I sink or swim? Do I run or stand up and fight? I am here to tell you that you are a superhero!

The thing we love about superheroes is they all have a knack for finding trouble. But they also have a knack for stepping up and overcoming against all odds and adversities. No matter how great the obstacle, superheroes always come out on top. Many of us even think it would be nice if we had superpowers like our favorite heroes.

Do you know why superheroes always come out on top, though? It's not necessarily because of the wonderful superpowers they have. The superhero's true power does not lie in the special abilities they possess, because their villains often have even greater abilities. That's not the thing that makes a superhero win. It's the belief in their heart that they can come out on top, and it's the resolve to never quit.

I know you've been waiting desperately for so long for someone or something to step in and save the day. You've been waiting for your Superman or your Wonder Woman to come in and fight with everything they have to overcome your adversity. But I'm here to tell you that the hero that you're anxiously waiting to come lies buried deep inside of you. You are that hero.

In order to see that manifest in your life, like the heroes we talked about before, you have to resolve right now, this very moment, to never quit. Never give up. No matter how dark the skies above you may seem, the clouds will always pass by and the sun will shine on your life again. Regardless of how hopeless your situation may seem you are never without hope. As long as there's a heart beating inside your chest, you have the ability to accomplish great things in this world.

Your superpower is your mindset that says, "I am the hero in my story, and I will not give up!" It doesn't matter how big the mountain is in front of you, and I understand there are some extremely big mountains in this world. Because you are a superhero, you have the strength. Life built you for this very mountain. All of your past experiences, the hateful people, the evil you see so readily around you, have been preparing you. Everything you've ever experienced, good and especially bad, led you to this moment to strengthen you for the climb.

You can accomplish this because you are a hero. It's commitment time. I need you to make a promise both to me and more importantly to yourself. I need you to vow that you will not give up no matter what. When you give up, you ruin your chance to experience the happy ending. When you allow circumstances to take the zeal, zest, and fervor out of you, you negate the positive outcome. If you don't allow the hero to be activated and instead let it lie dormant inside of you, you cancel your success story.

You have to decide to stand up and show up. You have to fight with everything inside of you day after day after day until your miracle happens. Because your miracle will happen. Your story will end well, and you will come out on top. That's when everything you've ever gone through will be worthwhile and you will understand it all. Promise yourself right now to never give up, and then the sky's the limit. From here, there's nowhere to go but up. It's time to fully become the hero of your own life. Why? Because YOU CAN.

Vital Reflections to Discuss or Journal:

1. *Who is your favorite superhero? What characteristics do you most love about them? How do you personally identify with these characteristics?*

2. *Have you ever wished someone would step in and save the day for you in your life?*

3. *We all love good stories. Why is it so easy to root for your favorite character in your favorite story yet so difficult for you believe in your own ability to save the day in your life?*

4. *You are the hero you've so desperately wished would step in and save the day. What steps will you take moving forward to rise up and become the hero in your own epic life story?*

Chapter 7

WHAT'S (SELF)LOVE GOT TO DO WITH IT?

You have identified the problem and awoken from your slumber, and your wheels are beginning to turn as it pertains to taking back control of your life. Now it's time for us to truly dig in deep and start getting really practical here. Throughout the remainder of this book, we will be discovering the power that you have to take back control of the wheel of your life in order to build the life that you love to live.

In order to do this, nothing else is more important than this first and primary step: you must learn to practice self-love. You can't effectively do anything or give anything of substance back into the world until you begin practicing self-love. I know this sounds easy, but it's actually more difficult than it sounds. This is an area that everyone struggles with in some capacity.

No matter how narcissistic you may think a person seems, deep down when they get alone, there is at least one area of their life where they have doubts. Where they have fears and begin to believe that they may not be good enough or have what it takes to make it in this world. But in order for you to give love, give life, and truly live fulfilled, you must learn to love yourself.

I recall a time when I was traveling to Australia. And for a person who does not enjoy flying, I certainly have a lot of airplane analogies. If you've flown before, regardless of where you're going, you know that moment when you board the plane. Everyone is rushing around to place their bags in the overhead bin and looking for their seat. You're hoping to get an aisle seat, or a window seat, or perhaps even a seat to yourself. At the very least, you're hoping to get a seat by someone who's nice. If you've flown before, you know you've been there.

Before you can take off, the flight attendants have to go through a spiel. It's the same on every flight, and you may even be able to repeat it if you've flown enough. The purpose of the announcement is to inform you of what to do in case of an emergency. The attendant makes sure you know where all the emergency exits are located and that the seats can be used as a flotation device. You are told that if the cabin were to lose air pressure for any reason, oxygen masks will drop from the ceiling. A demonstration of how to properly use the mask follows this, along with the part of the announcement that I find the most important. It is of the utmost priority that you secure your own mask first.

The idea of this is difficult for me. I have small children, and it's hard to even fathom trying to save myself before my child. But this is why it's so important. If you are trying to secure a mask on someone else and have problems, chances are both of you will pass out. Then, everyone loses. That's why it's so important for you to secure your mask first so that you can help as many people as possible. You can never truly and completely help anyone else until you've learned to help yourself first. You can't save anyone else if you don't save yourself first.

I can't think of a more powerful analogy as it pertains to our lives and loving ourselves. So often we give love freely to all those around us, but we struggle most when it comes to loving ourselves. The reality is, self-love is hard. We've all collected a lot of baggage along the way, starting in our child-hood, all the way up to this very moment. Because of this, self-love takes energy and effort, and it will tire you out at times. It can be exhausting.

On the flipside of this, you may not only be lacking in self-love. You may be indulging in self-hate, which also has harmful effects. Self-hate comes across differently and is actually easy to do in the moment, and the lasting effects are even more harm-ful than lack of self-love. Either way, you have a hard choice to make. And, let me reassure you. You have to choose your heart when it comes to this situation.

You cannot truly give all of your love to anyone else – not your spouse, your child, another family member, a pet, not to anyone – until you learn to love yourself, flaws and all. I know it's much easier said than done because there are rude people who exist in this world. There are angry people, hurt people, and unhappy people who seem to exist for the sole purpose of making your life a nightmare.

This makes you feel unloved and unwanted. You end up thinking that you're not enough, and after a while, you begin to take in and believe those thoughts and feelings that others put upon you. You begin to carry it with you and walk in those beliefs. Eventually, it causes your eyes to become weary. Your soul becomes weak and drained, and you fall asleep at the wheel.

In order for you to wake up and take back control, you need to understand a fundamental truth. There's nothing wrong with who you are. You didn't do anything to cause this or deserve this. Those people who make you feel less than and as if you're not enough do so because of how badly they feel about themselves. We've all heard those old sayings, and they ring true even today. Misery loves company, and hurt people hurt people.

Never allow hurt or miserable people and their words to affect how you think and feel about yourself. Realize that as people, we are all the same. We all breathe the same air. We all get dressed the same way in the mornings. Everyone has the same basic needs of food for nourishment and sleep.

The biggest threat to learning to love yourself is the need for validation from our peers. Unfortunately, this internal need often resurrects the monster comparison that we dealt with earlier. In order to move forward successfully, it's important to realize these truths.

No one is exempt from pain and hurt. No one is exempt from struggle and loss. So, while you're busy comparing yourself and your perceived shortcomings to someone else, there is someone else who is looking at you. They're idolizing your life and coveting everything you have. They're wishing they could trade places with you, not knowing the extent of the hurt and pain you've gone through. Not seeing how difficult it was for you to get where you are, and not knowing that you're still not where you hope to be in this life.

In order for you to build your ideal life, you must begin to love and appreciate the uniqueness of your own journey. And yes, that includes the mountain tops and the highs of life. It includes the love and the moment you said, "I do." It includes the moment where you witnessed the birth of your first child, and you saw their beautiful eyes looking back at you. It includes those moments of major accomplishments when you graduated from high school, or university, or when you received your master's degree or your PhD. It's comprised of all your mountain highs.

But you also have to learn to appreciate the valley lows. That's where it becomes difficult because no one likes the struggles that come with life. It's difficult, but it's hard for a reason. Where you have to shift your perspective is in realizing that the struggle is for your benefit. It's only going to lead to the strength that it takes for you to continue to climb more mountains and experience more peaks in this life.

There was a song that was written a few years back, and it's actually one of my favorite songs. I know many people feel different ways about the artist, but you can't take away from the fundamental truths in this song. It's by the urban/country philosopher Miley Cyrus, and she penned a song called The Climb. This song really resonates with me. It always has, and it always will. The lyrics read:

I can almost see it
That dream I'm dreaming but
There's a voice inside my head saying
You'll never reach it,

Every step I'm taking,
Every move I make feels
Lost with no direction
My faith is shaking but I
Gotta keep trying
Gotta keep my head held high

There's always gonna be another mountain
I'm always gonna wanna make it move
Always gonna be an uphill battle
Sometimes I'm gonna have to lose
Ain't about how fast I get there
Ain't about what's waiting on the other side
It's the climb

When I think about these words, it makes me think about actual mountains. I've been fortunate enough to explore several mountains. I've been to the mountains in Wyoming, California, Colorado, and New Mexico. I've also explored the Great Smoky Mountains in Tennessee where I'm from and the Appalachians a little further north in Pennsylvania. Mountains are beautiful, but the process of getting on top of the mountains is not always so beautiful. As a matter of fact, there were moments where my breath was literally taken away in fear at what I was seeing and the possibility of tumbling over the side.

But do you know what makes the view from the top of a mountain so worth it? It's not just the view you get to see and take in, but it's the journey that it took to get there. I'm not a climber, but I have many friends who are, and I've done it before. I didn't enjoy it, but that's a story for another day. What you realize is that the thing that makes the summit of the mountain that much sweeter is the struggle it took to get there. It's every time you looked at what seemed like an impossible task and thought, 'I can't do it.' When you thought, 'I don't have what it takes to make it,' and every time you slipped and almost fell. It's every time you felt like giving up, but you chose not to. That is what makes the moment that much sweeter when you get to the top.

That is the same thing that comes with your life. When you're in those not so beautiful moments of your life and you're in the valley lows, you have to know that the climb it takes you to get back out is what makes your mountain highs that much sweeter. It's you stepping into that role that we discussed in the last chapter of fully becoming the hero of your own life. It's you waking up, taking control of the wheel, and moving forward with purpose as you learn to love yourself.

We will continue to build a plan throughout the remainder of this book to help you to truly love the life that you live. In order to do so, it's time to get practical. Maybe you don't know where to start with loving yourself, so I'm going to give you a few practical things to do to begin taking steps. There are several things you can do, but I want you to know right away that it takes commitment. Commitment means that you have to stay true and loyal. You have to stay focused on what you said you were going to do long after that feeling in which you said it passes.

I know it's easy for me to say I'm going to be focused. I promise myself I'm going to hit the gym five days a week and

I'm going to eat well. It's easy to say that when I'm motivated. But days, weeks, months later, am I still committed to that? Am I still choosing to do what I said I was going to do, even though the motivation has gone? That's what you need to realize. Self-love takes tremendous commitment. Even on the days when you feel bad, when you feel like you're not enough, and when you feel less than, you're still going to have to put in the work, effort, and practice. That's how you create your new reality.

After you've made a commitment to yourself in your heart, the first step I want you to take to learn how to love yourself is to practice daily affirmations. Affirmations are telling yourself new truths, fundamental truths that you choose to live by. I have my own, but I'm not going to share them now because this needs to be personal to you. The only way to get the most out of it is for you to make it personal.

You have to think specifically about where you feel you fall short in life. Maybe you feel worthless. If that's the case, you have to create an affirmation to counteract that feeling, something like, 'I am worth more than the most precious resources in the world.' Perhaps you feel like you're not smart because you've been told your whole life that you're stupid. You have to say to yourself, 'I am smart. I am intelligent. And I am capable of learning and accomplishing new and important things.'

These are just a couple examples. Whatever it is that makes you feel like you're not enough, you need to create an affirmation that directly contradicts that feeling. You then need to say it to yourself out loud every day. I'm going to be honest with you. It's likely going to feel silly at first, but it's not about how it makes you feel in the moment. It's about how it begins to shift your mindset and your heart over time once you've created a new foundation of who you are.

The next practical step you need to take, and it's actually a big one, is to stop the negative self-talk. I can't tell you how many times I hear people talk badly about themselves. Even in small moments where they maybe make a mistake, I hear them say things like, 'I'm so stupid,' or, 'I'm such an idiot.' I even hear them say, 'I hate myself.' You may do the same thing.

When you say these things, you don't realize the power those words carry. Even though you say them half-heartedly and probably don't fully mean them in the moment, you still said the words and feel them in your heart. They're tucked back into the crevices of your mind, ready to creep back in at a later time when you need confidence. Only now you feel horrible about yourself because you've learned to treat yourself so badly. You freely practice kindness to other people and show them the utmost grace when they make a mistake. Yet you don't extend the same level of grace and mercy to yourself. Instead you beat yourself down and take away the very life and love that you could possibly have.

You must stop negative self-talk. I can't stress enough how vital it is to stop saying negative things about yourself. When you feel it happening, force yourself to stop mid-thought. If you have a slip up and yell it out without thinking, that's okay. Give yourself a break and understand it's okay to make mistakes. It's okay to be imperfect but continue that commitment to loving yourself. Continue to work at stopping the negative self-talk because that's a huge pillar of learning to love yourself.

The third practical step is to practice gratitude regularly. As a matter of fact, you need to practice gratitude daily. You need to reflect on what you are grateful for. You're unhappy so many times in life because you don't realize how much you truly have. You don't see how awesome your life truly is, even when you don't feel that way.

When you're going through something, it's hard to see the beauty of it at the time. For example, if you went into the Amazon rainforest in the middle of a bog or Mississippi in the middle of a swamp, it might feel and look dirty, murky, dark, damp, and ugly. But if you stepped out and found a way to climb a cliff and overlook that very same forest or swamp, you could see it in its entirety and marvel at the beauty that exists within it.

Sometimes you need to do the same thing in your own life. When you're in it every single day, it's difficult to see the beauty of it because you're too busy in the middle of it. You need to find a time that works for you, whether early in the morning or right before you fall asleep and make a list every day of all that you're grateful for. Then spend time reflecting on that list. I promise it will warm your heart. When you intentionally practice gratitude, your mind will be blown at just how remarkable your life truly is, even in the not so fun chapters.

Commit to do these three things, and I guarantee you are well on your way to taking back control of the wheel and building the life you love to live. None of the steps are huge things.

They're simple things that you can implement today. This is not a whole plan. If you want a whole plan, I'm always available. You can reach out to me and we can talk later. But for now, these are things you can start doing this very moment that you can take with you, regardless of where you are in the world as you read this.

Now that we've fully explored ways to love yourself and seen how large of a pillar that is foundationally for everything else we want to build on, we continue to progress forward. We now need to also recognize a close cousin of self-love that is similar but not exactly the same. It's self-investment. Self-investment has more to do with ways you pour into yourself to continue to grow, whether that be personally, relationally, professionally, or spiritually. It's important to invest in yourself.

One of the things I've been fortunate to learn over the last few years through work I've put in, through mentors, and through people who have poured into me, is that leaders are life-long learners. That's a fundamental truth. If you didn't know it already, I'm here to let you know that you are a leader. John Maxwell's definition of leadership is influence. Everybody has influence over at least one other person in their life, which means you, my friend, are a leader.

In order to be the best possible leader, steward your life well, and get the most out of your life, you need to continue to learn. Leaders are learners and it is a life-long process of learning. It doesn't matter if you're reading this book and you're a pre-teen, in your 30s, in your 80s sitting on the porch in your rocker reflecting on the beautiful life that you've had and all the loved ones you've been fortunate enough to share moments and memories with, or anywhere in-between. Regardless of where you find yourself in that spectrum, you are a leader and you can never stop learning.

That's why you're reading this book right now. I am thankful to you, my friend, for not sacrificing yourself and for choosing to invest in you. But for many people, believe it or not, this is actually a struggle. I know a lot of times when you think about investing in yourself you struggle because you're busy. Life is busy. It moves at the pace of the fast and the furious.

There are things that continue to pop up day after day. Your calendar is overrun with events that you sometimes have to say no to even when you don't want to because you're so busy running back and forth with kids. Perhaps you're a college student and you're running yourself ragged with courses and extracurriculars. Maybe you're overrun with your job, family priorities, and even fun. Where's leisure? We've got to throw that in there somewhere, too.

The point I'm trying to make is that everyone is busy. One of the things that hurts my heart is that so many times you will invest in everything and everyone except yourself. I've seen it over and over again in people I've coached and talked with personally. You are willing to invest in everything else first before investing in yourself. I know this because there was a time in my life when I did this as well.

I shared the story with you about how I let myself go and ended up getting diagnosed with diabetes. I did go on to overturn that diagnosis because I made the decision to fight for my life. That is what you are choosing right now. But I'm here to tell you it isn't going to be easy and will likely require some sacrifices on your part.

When I made the decision to fight for my life, I had to make some choices and think about finding some coaches, people who were experts in areas where I was not. One of the first places I found was a fat-loss camp dedicated to helping people take back control of their lives physically. I went to a meeting and heard about how wonderful and how successful the program was and the ways that it worked. After hearing this, I was like, 'Where do I sign up?'

As the meeting continued, I couldn't wait to sign on the dotted line. But then they went over the particulars of the cost of the program, and I'm not going to lie, the number that was spit out was enough to blow my mind. There was no way I could ever afford something that expensive. We wouldn't be able to survive if I paid that amount of money.

And then it hit me. I was telling myself that it was too expensive, that I'd never be able to afford it, but I had no problem spending that same amount of money or more on other things. I spent money on events and travel. I spent that same amount or more eating out over the year, investing in other people's restaurants and dreams. I spent money throughout the year giving to other friends and other people's business ventures.

I willingly spent my resources on everything else, but when it came time when I actually needed to invest in myself, I was hesitant. That is when I made a choice. My life was worth it. I needed to pull the trigger and make that investment in myself.

And as you read in the previous chapter, it was that initial investment that I made in myself that helped me officially reverse the diagnosis of diabetes.

I understand that giving to others is often easier than giving to yourself. It's easier to support a friend and their dream. It's easier to support local businesses and shops or even people in other countries and mission work. All those things are good. You very well should do those things because giving is something that is important for us to do. However, you cannot invest in everything else and forget to invest in yourself. In fact, you need to learn to invest in yourself first.

You make actual investments and pay everyone but yourself. You pay all the bills, all these different companies and corporations. You pay for every single thing, and if you don't have a savings account, you're paying everyone but yourself. I had a mentor tell me, "I refuse to ever pay all my money out to everyone else in the world and leave nothing for myself." So, as a believer, after he returned to God what was His, he made the choice to pay himself. Then he paid all the bills.

The point I'm making is that you invest in everything else but you. You need to realize, though, that you matter, and you are worth the investment in yourself. I have had to find coaches in several areas of my life, and I'll be honest with you. They always come with a price. But I've decided that in order for me to live my best life and give the most effective version of myself to the world, my beautiful wife and lovely boys, my friends, family, and all those I hold dear, I must invest in myself to maximize my potential.

What area of your life have you slacked off in and not invested in yourself? What area have you been feeling that you need to grow, and you desperately need help? Maybe you need to see a therapist because you need someone to talk with and help you process things you've gone through. Possibly you need a financial planner because you need to flip the current way that you've handled your finances on its head. Perhaps you need a fitness coach so that you can take back control of your life physically. Or maybe you need pastoral counseling to help in finding your way spiritually.

No matter what area it is, you need to make the choice to invest in yourself regardless of the cost. You need to internalize that you are worth it. It's time to prioritize you, because when you do this, you can maximize your life. When you become better, everything else around you becomes better, including your marriage, your family, your career, and your overall life. Choose today to invest in yourself. Why? Because you can!

Vital Reflections to Discuss or Journal:

1. *Have you ever struggled with loving yourself? What part of you is most difficult for you to love? Why do you think that is?*

2. *How do you plan to eliminate negative self-talk?*

3. *Why is it important to invest in yourself? What area(s) of your life do you plan on focusing on to invest in yourself this year?*

4. *How can learning to love yourself unconditionally change your life for the better?*

5. *List your new daily affirmations. Spend at least 5 minutes practicing them now.*

Chapter 8

THE INCREDIBLE
POWER OF CHOICE

Now that you realize the importance of loving yourself and are fully committed to the process of doing so, it's time to discover a superpower that has the potential to transform your entire life – the incredible power of choice. The choices you make determine everything in your life. Statistics have shown that the average person makes about 35,000 choices every single day. The life you live is directly dictated by those very choices. The superpower, then, is learning the ability to make the best choice possible.

The first thing you need to do is forgive yourself for the bad choices that have led you into unfavorable situations. Maybe you feel as if you're a bad person and that you're too far gone to ever come back. Perhaps you believe that you've done too much damage through the choices of your life and you feel helpless and hopeless and don't know where to begin to move forward. If you find yourself in that place, the first thing I want to tell you is that there are no good or bad people. You are not a bad person; there are only good and bad choices.

The choices that you make are typically determined by your life experiences and the environment in which you grew up. No matter who a person is, everyone has a part of them that longs to be innately good, that longs to be back with God, that longs for health, life, and love. But when you have been in certain situations or environments for far too long, it slowly begins to deteriorate the level of choices available, and you begin to make bad choices.

In this chapter, I want to give you a few vital tools to help you make the best choices every day of your life, choices that will begin to shift the entire trajectory of your life. The first is the most important choice, and you need to make it right now, this very moment. You must choose to stop feeling sorry for yourself and stop playing the victim. I'm definitely not referring to people who are actual victims. We live in a world where evil exists and there are people who are victimizing others, and I completely understand. If that's you, you should definitely speak up, reach out, and seek help immediately.

But that's not the person I'm talking to. I'm talking to those of you who have grown comfortable and complacent in sitting in the middle of your situation. I'm talking to the person who is always sad and thinks every single day is a bad day. I'm addressing the person who never accepts responsibility for where you are in life, the 'woe is me' type who always thinks that everything that has gone wrong in life is someone else's fault.

In order for you to become who you're meant to be, you must learn to take personal responsibility for your actions and where you are in life. You need to understand that in your life, you can only control what you can control. Maybe it's not your fault. You may have been led into a situation because of someone else's choices. It could be there were things that were completely out of your control, and life has taken advantage of you, backed you into a corner, and pressed you up against a wall. But while that may be someone else's fault, it's no one else's fault but your own if you choose to stay there.

Remember, you are the hero of this story because it's yours. This is your story, so stop waiting on someone else to come in, sweep through, and save the day. Don't expect someone else to fix everything because that is not going to happen. If you ever want to build a life that you love to live, it starts the day that you accept your situation for what it is – the good, the bad, the ugly, and everything else in between. You have to make the choice to stop feeling sorry for yourself and pick up the pieces to start moving forward.

The day that you make this choice is the day that you become free. It's the day you truly free yourself from the bondage of an unhappy and unfulfilled life. If you find yourself in a place where you are feeling sorry for yourself, it's okay. We're all human and no one is perfect. We've all been there. I've been there. I'm not coming down on you or fussing at you, so don't feel isolated or alone. I only know that there's more inside of you, and I want to help you unlock the power to get to your passion, potential, and purpose in this life.

I know what it's like to be diagnosed with a life-altering and potentially life-threatening disease. I know what it feels like to have your heart stomped into the ground and broken into a million pieces, having no idea where to begin picking up those pieces. I understand what it's like to lose someone that you so desperately love that it leaves a hole the size and shape of them in your heart forever. I've experienced deep hurt and pain in this life, but I also know what it feels like to stand up and begin picking up the pieces, taking slow steps which are much better than no steps. I've been able to press on even when I felt like I couldn't, and I know you can, too.

You know how I know this? Because you are the hero of your story. I know sometimes life may not seem fair. I would never sit here and try to tell you that life is fair, but then again, no one ever promised that it would be fair. If someone ever made you that promise, shame on them because that's sadly not the case. Making the choice to stop feeling sorry for yourself will not be easy, especially if you're accustomed to sitting in your circumstances. Know that nothing worth having in this life ever comes easy.

When I reflect on my own life, none of my greatest accomplishments ever came easy. Dating and winning the heart of my wife took effort. The process of bringing children into this world wasn't easy, especially for my wife. Stepping out on faith in my career was not easy. My career path has not been smooth because I've had to leave my comfort zone, taking new steps while ending old ones. Even writing this book is not easy. But it's all been more than worth the effort that it requires because it's so fulfilling.

In order for you to take the next step in your life, you must commit to keep going, continue growing, and start taking steps to pick up the pieces. Remember, whether it's your fault or not, you need to take responsibility for the steps you are taking this day. It's time for you to start moving, my friend.

The second choice that you can make is also one of the most important. You must choose to surround yourself with the right people. I'll never forget a day many years ago when I was in college at Oklahoma Christian University. I had an elementary ministry class on teaching children about the foundations of faith. This particular day, there was a paper on everyone's desk as we entered the classroom. The paper said the word 'FRIENDS' in large, bubble letters.

After everyone sat, the teacher passed out No. 2 pencils. Not mechanical pencils, but old-school, real No. 2 pencils. They had been sharpened by hand in one of those antique metal thingies that used to sit on a desk. For those of us of a certain age, you know what I'm talking about, but my children will never have the pleasure of experiencing one of these. It was called a pencil sharpener, and the teacher had hand-cranked each pencil to a nice, pointed tip.

The teacher told us to use the pencils to color in the bubble letters on the paper. As we were coloring, she began to tell a story about the importance of choosing the right people to walk with on this journey called life. After about 10 minutes, the teacher asked if everyone was done coloring, which we were. "This is what I want you to do," she said, "I want you to take your paper, put it face down on your arm and begin rubbing it in." We were all puzzled. Was she serious? What was the purpose? She could

ASLEEP AT THE WHEEL: TAKING BACK CONTROL OF YOUR LIFE

see the confusion on our faces and continued, "Trust me. Just do it."

One by one, we each took our papers and began rubbing them on our arms. I didn't notice anything on my own arm at first because I was looking at a friend, but I could see the lead smearing all over her skin. Then I looked at my own arm and to my surprise it had done the same thing to me; I had smudges of lead from the picture all over my arm. It was about this time that light bulbs started going off in heads all around the room. The teacher said, "See, it's very important to choose the right people in this life to walk with you, because friends rub off on you." Her demonstration worked perfectly. The word 'FRIENDS' on the paper had indeed rubbed off on all of us.

The community around you can literally suck the life out of you and pull you down, or they can pour life into you and build you up. If you have a horrible attitude, or you're angry and upset every day, check the people who are in your circle. If every day is filled with shame, drama, and gossip about other people and their life experiences, check your surroundings. It's likely affected directly by the people you have in your ears, those closest to you.

If you ever want real peace, support, and prosperity in your life, you must surround yourself with people who value those same things. There are fountains, and every fountain has a drain at the bottom of it. Fountains pour out non-stop into everything around them. Do you know what drains do? They only exist to sit there and suck up what the fountain is pouring out.

The question then is, are you surrounding yourself with fountains or drains? Are you surrounding yourself with people who are pouring into you, filling you with life, and building you up, or are you surrounding yourself with people who have set themselves to drain out the very life that you pour into this world? If you want to build a solid foundation in which you have accountability, friendship, love, and community, it starts with you making wise choices in choosing those people you surround yourself with.

Another choice that you need to make regularly in life is to serve those around you. The road to healing is directly tied to living a life of service. We already discussed earlier how hurt people have a tendency to hurt people, as the saying goes. But I've also heard it said that healed people help people. If you are a person that has been healed or you're on the road to healing, one of the primary ways you can help that process along is to begin helping others heal, as well.

You shouldn't serve others for what you can get, but for what you give, instead. I see so many people who want to help others for the accolades. They want a platform, to be recognized, or to be on the news, *The Ellen Show* or *Oprah*. It shouldn't be about that. Those things are byproducts of what happens out of a heart of servitude when you choose service. They shouldn't be the reason you serve.

I've served with multiple missions, both here in cities all around the United States and in other countries abroad. I can tell you from personal experience that when you choose to place others ahead of yourself, when you choose a life of service, and you choose to commit to pouring into those around you, it literally transforms your entire life from the inside out. Your heart that has grown cold, tired and weary, will begin to warm up and open up again. You begin to have hope again as the light begins to go off in your eyes and you start to see the positive impact you can have in this world.

There's nothing that can prepare you for the feeling that comes when you see a family experience true love and gratitude because of your hands, because you helped serve them in a time that they needed it most. You are able to see the good of humanity, again. It can lead to feeling better physically, as well as improving your mood as you feel connected to something greater than yourself.

When the world revolves around you, that's a very sad and lonely place. It's a setup for disappointment. As one of my mentors Jason Morris would say, "When you're the center of your universe, that's a terrible place to be." He went on to explain that you would always be let down, sad, and upset. However, when you are centered on service and serving those around you, pouring back and giving into them, that is when real life and real love happens. Your heart will be in a beautiful place.

Every time I've ever served a mission or done any type of service to those around me, it creates a feeling deep down at the soul level, a feeling that I'm making a difference in the world. As a believer in Christ, that is so important. If you are a believer, you know that Jesus came here and walked this earth for the sole purpose of serving those around Him and saving them.

He is the ultimate example of how to be servants. We serve one another because it is directly tied to our purpose for being here.

That's also when you will feel most alive. Every time you serve another person, it gives you a feeling like nothing else. Your mind has been centered around yourself. I know that switching your mind to begin serving others might not be the easiest choice to make. I'm not telling you that you should hop on a plane and fly to South America. I'm not suggesting that you go to Mexico or Africa or any other country in the world. You don't even have to go to the impoverished areas of the city you're in before you begin serving.

Service starts right now where you are, whether you're in an office or in your car. Whether you're at home in bed, at the dinner table, or out shopping. No matter where you are at this exact moment, service starts now. You have the opportunity to serve those around you. My encouragement to you is to start small. In what ways can you serve your spouse better? How can you make their day a little bit better for them by making their load a little bit lighter?

Serve your children. In what ways can you serve your children and teach them about what real, genuine love looks like? Serve your coworkers. I know they might have horrible attitudes. Perhaps they mistreat you and look down on you. But I guarantee you, you have the power to transform that environment if you begin to serve them. They may respond harshly at first, but no one would continue to do so once they see that you're not doing it for a response; you're doing it out of your heart to love and care for those around you.

When you make this choice, it transforms everything around you for the positive. Always choose life, love, and happiness. These are words I say quite often, but what does that actually mean? To choose life means to choose the things in this world that make you feel most alive. What are the things that literally make you feel awake, fulfilled, joyful, and present? Those are the things you need to choose more of every single day. If you don't know what those things are, we'll get into a process later to help you. But for now, start by thinking about the things that make you feel most alive and write them down because you need to know how to answer that question.

You also need to always choose love. It was Dr. Martin Luther King Jr., who said, "Darkness cannot drive out darkness; only light can do that. Hate cannot drive out hate; only love can do that." Those are powerful words because love has the ability to overpower all the evil and darkness in this world combined. I guarantee that in your own life, you will never transform things into a positive manner by responding in a negative way. To see things improve in a positive way it's going to take you making the choice to love those around you.

Always choose happy. Happiness is a choice, and it takes the power of perspective for you to realize just how much of a choice your happiness is. So often we focus on what we do not have rather than what we do have. All we see is our deficiencies in life and our shortcomings. But when you begin to practice gratitude like we discussed earlier, then you can begin to understand exactly what you do have, the riches you have. You can then begin to choose to be happy.

When you make the choice when you wake up in the morning that it's going to be a good day, those words have power. And guess what? You may still have a tire blow out on the way to work. Someone may still cut you off or almost run you off the road. You may still have to deal with the horrible attitudes of your coworkers or even your own children. Regardless of what circumstances you face, you've already decided in your mind that it's going to be a good day, and you've chosen to be happy. You'll notice it's almost as if you've put on a special cloak that allows all the negative things to roll right off you. Practice choosing to be happy every day. Whether you believe it or not, tell yourself every day, 'It's going to be a good day and I will be happy.'

As we come to the conclusion of this chapter, I want to leave you with a couple things I've learned along my journey. I call them the Golden Questions. There are only two, but these two questions have helped me make almost every single choice I need to make because they pertain to things so much greater than my current circumstance. Let me explain where I got these questions.

I enjoy spending a lot of time with older people. I like having older mentors, and I have many older people I spend time with regularly who pour into my life. There's a wealth of wisdom that comes from people who have so much life experience and stories to offer. I would suggest that if you don't already, you should spend time with older people. Don't ever look at older individuals as less than because they may not be able to help themselves in every area. They've lived a long life and can teach you a thing or two if you're open to learning. Remember, leaders are learners.

In spending time with my older mentors, I began to ask them questions like, 'What have you learned in life? If you could go back and change anything, what would it be? What is the greatest piece of advice you can give me?' These two golden questions came out of the responses I received from multiple people.

So, the first question is, 'When you come to the end of your journey and find yourself on your deathbed, how much is this going to matter to you then?' The "this" in the question is whatever circumstance you're currently facing. I've used this when I've had to make choices, like how to respond to my wife in times of heated discussion where we're both passionate about a particular thing. We could easily go down the wrong path of fussing and arguing, which we don't like to do. When this happens, I think and ask the question, 'How much is whatever we're passionately discussing going to matter to us on our deathbed?'

Think about this in every area of your life. Think about it when there are things that upset you, that take your life away and bring you down. Consider this question when things cause you to have extreme frustration, anger, worry, anxiety, or fear. Contemplate this as it pertains to your family, friends, colleagues, your job, other people's opinions and perspectives of you, and all of the other things that we allow to dictate our lives.

How much is whatever you're facing going to matter to you when you're on your deathbed and getting ready to leave this world? If the answer to that question is not very much then, the answer to that question needs to be not very much now. You have to make the switch. We're as practical as practical can be right now. The next time you face an adverse situation or circumstance that makes you feel anger, frustration, or any negative emotion that weighs you down to where you no longer see the path to move forward, I want you to ask yourself that question. In the grand scheme of your life how much is this going to matter?

If the answer is not very much then, it should completely alter your perspective. No one knows when their number will be called. Prayerfully it's many years from now for all of us, but the reality is that's not the case. Why waste valuable time and precious moments of your life, that you'll never get back, on something that isn't going to matter to you when it's your time to be called away from this life? Those are words to live by.

The second Golden Question that I again learned from my older mentors is, 'What is my goal, and is this response going to get me closer or further away from that goal?' I have many goals in this life. One of my goals is to be a great dad to my sons. I want them to love me and look up to me. I want them to know that I loved them, cared for and supported them, and that I gave them a foundation on which they could build.

Sometimes life gets heavy. My job gets hard and stress begins to pull me down and weigh heavily on me. I begin to get anxious and nervous about all the things going on in my life. At those times, when my kids are just being kids, maybe being loud, flipping and tumbling around the house or breaking things, my natural response may be to jump up, yell and scream. But I have to stop and ask myself, 'What is my goal?'

I then remind myself that my goal is to be a great father. To teach them discipline and instill in them a great foundation. If I yell and scream, berate and belittle my children, is that going to get me closer to my goal as a father or further away? The answer is further away, which means I shouldn't make that choice. I know that seems difficult in the moment when it's heated, but I promise you can do it. It just takes practice. Remember, practice doesn't make perfect. There's no such thing as perfection. Practice makes permanent.

My wife and I don't argue a whole lot. I'm thankful that we have built a wonderful relationship over the years filled with love. But in the beginning, that wasn't so much the case. The foundation of love was always there, but you have to learn to live with another individual who has an entirely different way of doing things than yourself. Heated moments would come, and we would be fussing at each other. My goal has always been to be a wonderful, loving husband and to never let divorce be an option.

When you're fussing and fighting, though, you can be tempted to use ugly and hurtful words to hurt the other person. It's not something you want to do, but it just happens sometimes in the heat of the moment. That's when I have to pause and ask myself, 'What is my goal for my marriage? Is me saying those words in the moment going to get me further or closer to my goal?' Again, if the answer is further away, I need to make a different choice.

These questions have the power to change your entire life if you implement them and allow them to. When you are in the middle of a choice you need to make, take time to ask yourself these questions. 'How much is this going to matter to you in the grand scheme of your life?' If it's a lot, then you need to take your time to thoroughly weigh all your options. If your answer is the opposite, (not very much), you don't need to waste time, energy, or effort in your valuable life on something that's not going to make a difference to you in the end.

Secondly, what is your goal? What do you want in this life? What do you want for your marriage? What do you want for your family? What do you want for your career? What do you want in your faith walk? What do you want in your fitness journey? Are the choices you're making going to get you closer to or further away from your goals? If the answer is closer, then friend, you're making the right choice. But if the answer is further away, you need to stop right now in your tracks because that is not the choice for you.

Vital Reflections to Discuss or Journal:

1. *Do you ever feel overwhelmed by the amount of choices you have to make on a daily basis? How do you typically handle the stress and pressure of your daily choices?*

2. *Have you forgiven yourself for bad choices you've made in your life? If not, why not? How do you think forgiving yourself for bad choices will improve your life?*

3. *What type of friendships do you currently have? Are they life-giving relationships or do they drain and suck the life out of you? What type of choices do you need to make to ensure you are surrounded by the best supporting cast possible?*

4. *Choosing to serve others is one of the most rewarding decisions you could ever make. How does serving others affect your heart? How can you raise your serve in your community this year? Challenge: Find one event per quarter, locally or abroad, and give your time, talents, or treasure in service to your fellow man.*

5. *How can incorporating the golden questions into your thought process improve your communication, conflict resolution, and overall conflict resolution?*

Chapter 9

THE ROADMAP BACK TO YOU

What if I told you that I had the answer to all your problems? Literally every single headache or heartache that you have in this very moment, I have the answer to? What if I told you that all you have to do is go outside right now wherever you are, hop into your car and just head to Why? Or maybe you could just head over to No Name. Perhaps you could go to Why Not. Or maybe even head over to Pray. Just go do that. The answer to all of your problems are there. Go ahead. What are you waiting for? It's time for you to go. It's not just going to happen. You have to drive.

You may be incredibly confused right now as to what you just read. Maybe it would help you out a little if I told you that Why is a town in Arizona and No Name is in Colorado. Why Not is located in North Carolina, and the town of Pray can be found in Montana. That gives you a little more information and possibly even points you in the right direction. You could easily head towards Arizona, Colorado, North Carolina, or Montana, and you would be in the general area. But you will not get exactly what I promised you unless you find yourself in those specific towns. And the only way you're ever going to find these wonderfully named places is if you have a map.

Maps in life serve one of the most important purposes there are. If you're like me, many of us have become so dependent on maps we don't know what we'd do without them. GPS has become our best friend, with most of us having it built into our vehicles or on our smartphones. The concept of an actual paper map has almost become foreign. My children might not even recognize one if they saw it -or they might recognize it as an antique.

But the map is pivotal for this journey, because it is your directional guide to your destination. Maps make life easier, especially today's digital maps. There is this not so wonderful thing we have all experienced in life while driving. It's called construction. Digital maps have the ability to give you multiple route options for your destination, and they even take construction into consideration to tell you the fastest route.

Earlier this year, a few close friends and I took a long road trip across America to the wonderful Bay Area of California. We decided we wanted to take the scenic route in order to visit the Grand Canyon. None of us had ever been there before, and we thought it would be an incredible opportunity. When we got close, it was my turn to drive. I was unbelievably nervous because I have an extreme fear of heights and mountains. We'll get into those things another day. But as we discussed earlier it was not an option for me to allow that fear to hold me captive. It would not prevent me from experiencing life,

What we decided to do was pull up the wonderful digital map that is GPS and get directions to the Grand Canyon. It plainly told us that on one route, we would climb elevation at a much higher speed. On the other route, it would be a much slower climb. It would be a longer trip, but it would also be a much safer drive. To which I said, "Yeah, let's go with the longer route."

The map was able to give me comfort in knowing exactly where we were going, knowing which steps to take and when to take those steps. Maps take out all of the guesswork of arriving at your destination. It's an exact plan to get you from point A to point B.

This is something that is imperative if you're ever going to find yourself at your ultimate destination in life. If you're tired of going through the motions, tired of the way things have been, and sick and tired of being sick and tired, this is a vital part of the process. All you want is to live life and love it. Without a map to your destination, it's very easy for you to become lost. I'm certain that everyone reading these words has been lost at least once in their life. You may not have been terribly lost. You may have been just a little misguided or a little off track. But you were lost all the same.

Here's the thing about being lost. No one sets out upon any journey with the intention of getting lost. It doesn't work that way. Since we don't plan to become lost, when it happens, it's frustrating. Even more, depending on where you get lost or how far off course you find yourself, it can be very scary.

You were born into this world with passion and purpose and to accomplish great things. But somewhere along the way, with all of the things we've discussed, and all the different ways life can grab hold of you and distract you, you've lost your way. Maybe you've been too focused on things that don't matter, and now your eyelids are a little bit heavy. They will eventually become so heavy that it's hard to bear. Much like I did at the beginning of this book, you find yourself dozing off and slowly drifting away at the wheel of your life.

Having drifted away you begin to wake up. When you open your eyes you may very well not even recognize where you are in your life. Some of you reading these words in this very moment find yourself in this place. You don't know the person you've become or the life that you live. You don't recognize the people around you or have the slightest clue how you even began to get this far off track. You once knew what you wanted. Everything was in front of you. You were working hard and giving everything that you had to get to what you wanted.

Then life became too hard or too much to bear. You didn't have the support you needed, or perhaps you became distracted. Maybe you became complacent because life was good enough and you were okay with having a good enough life. But now you're coming to understand that there's still something lying inside of you that you haven't accomplished. You know you need to do it. You know, deep down, that you want to dig in and go and get it. I'm here to tell you exactly how to do that. No one wants to wind up lost or lonely, afraid and isolated from the things they once knew. It's time for us to change that and help you get back on track.

That is precisely why I've created the Vitalize process. Together in the next couple chapters, we're going to create your map which will take you directly to your ideal life. Together, we will create a vision plan that is completely customized to your deepest desires in order that we may set you on the path to a happier, but more importantly, a more fulfilling life. In order to do this, we have to discover one of the pillars that your vision plan in life will be built upon. That is the ever-important question, 'What do you want?'

Let me elaborate a little. As I'm talking about what you want it's not just what do you want right now. It's not about whether you want a soda or a burger. It has nothing to do with wanting to go to a movie. It's not about wanting to relax more or take a nap. That's not what we're talking about. I'm sure we all want those things.

What I mean is, what do you want most in this life? When you're 85 years old and in the twilight years of your life, sitting on your front porch in a rocking chair with a glass of sweet lemonade, as sweet as you can take, and you're reflecting over your life, what do you want to feel at that moment? What do you want your life to have spoken? What do you want your life to reflect? You have to be able to answer these questions.

The sad reality is that many of you couldn't tell me what you want. You could talk for 20 or 30 minutes and get around about, close to, and possibly tell me what you want generally. But if I asked you to tell me in just two or three sentences or three to five bullet points the keys or pillars that you want to accomplish overall in life, many of you couldn't do that. There are probably a couple reasons why you can't do that.

I've talked to and coached many people. As we've gone about this process and worked it out, a lot of people ask the question, 'Does it even matter what I want? Does anyone really care what I want?' That may be true. Many people in the world couldn't care less about what you want. It's not someone else's responsibility to care about that. It's your responsibility to identify, define, and care about what you want. If you've never spent time intentionally thinking through exactly what you want in this life, how can you ever expect to have a destination that you want to arrive at? How can you ever expect to feel fulfilled? How can you ever expect to love the life you live if you do not even know what you want?

Perhaps you're like another group of people who fall into the category of believers like me that wrestle deep down inside. You've been taught that what you want either doesn't matter or pales in comparison to what God wants for you. Because of this you've learned to not even think about what you want since what God wants for you is more important. I believe, though, that if you've given your heart to God and are living in submission to Him, what you want most in this life and what God wants most for you will intersect.

Those two will become one thing. Because your heart is in submission to Him, He is the one who created the desire that exists deep within you to begin with. That musical talent and wonderful voice you have and want to express, your athletic abilities, the splendid gift of planning and administration, the gift of listening and empathy, whatever it is... who do you think gave it to you? If God in heaven is the One who gave it to you, why then would He not want you to want that?

You need to know what you want in this life. If you ever hope to build a life that you love to live, it all starts by beginning to answer this question. Knowing what you want is the direct map to your final destination. It is the vision plan that leads directly to passion, purpose, and fulfillment.

Now it's time to get to work. Roll those sleeves up and get your pen out. It's time to create your map. I want you to take a few moments to reflect on what you want most in this life. What do you want to have accomplished, and what do you want your life to reflect? Now, on the next page you will see spaces. It's time for you to write it down.

You need to be very specific, not vague. It needs to be much more explicit than just saying you want to live a good life, or a happy life, or that you want to be a millionaire. You have to be much more precise. What specifically do you want? Nothing is off limits. You can't hope to know what you really want if you're not honest with yourself in this moment. So, take a few moments and write what you truly want in the space provided. Remember, the possibilities are endless so don't hold anything back. Feel free to continue writing in a notebook or journal if you need more space.

You've done it, my friend! That is the first step to your very own customized life vision plan. You know what you want, and now you know exactly where to aim. Now if I told you that everything you wanted in life existed in a particular destination, you have now identified that destination. Congratulations! It's time now to take it even a few steps deeper.

On the next couple pages, you'll find a diagram. I'm going to teach you exactly how to use it, because it's not enough to know what you want in life overall. To really identify exactly what you want and to then accomplish your life's goals, dreams, and mission, it's going to take you getting even deeper, deep diving a little lower in order to get down to the core of every area of your life. In order to maximize your life and truly reach your destination, it's going to take precise action steps and that's exactly where we're headed next.

In the center of the next page is an area where you can summarize what you just wrote in those paragraphs before. In two or three sentences or three to five bullet points, briefly summarize exactly what you wrote down as your greatest wants in life. After you've done this, you will move to the labeled boxes surrounding this central idea. For each area of your life listed, you need to repeat the same process we just completed above into subcategories listed.

Keep in mind, do not write down anything in your subcategories that is not in complete alignment with your overall central theme or mission that you listed in the main circle. Anything that doesn't fit with your overall mission is only pulling you further away from what you want. It is wasted sideways energy that will only distract you from your overall mission.

When you're making your list of wants within your subcategories, every single one of them needs to fit within your overall vision of what you want.

For ease, I've broken it down into four primary pillars that most human beings desire in life. For each, write down three to five words or sentences that summarize what you want. The first pillar is faith. Write down exactly what you want in your faith life. The next pillar is family. What do you want for your family life? What are your goals, not just right now, but for the long term? Next is finances. What do you want in your finances, and what do you want them to reflect when you come to the end of your days? And finally, what do you want in your health and fitness? What are your long-term objectives?

Maybe there are other areas in your life you'd like to identify that aren't represented by the four subcategories already listed. That's perfectly okay. I created this process to be 100% unique to you so you truly get the most out of this book and your life. You can have as many as you like. The more specific you are in this process, the better you'll be able to reach your destination. Now, go ahead and take a few minutes to fill in the diagram. To continue this process, you can fill in the diagram below, draw this diagram in a notebook or journal, or visit my website mblackspeaks.com to download the digital versions of this diagram for you to print and use at your leisure.

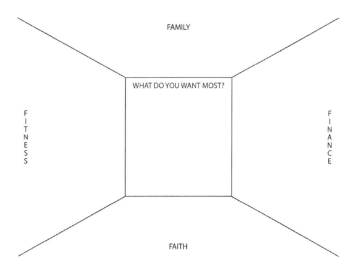

Now that you've finished filling in the diagram and established a concise map, you have really done it this time, my friend. You now have a very precise destination on your journey. You now have the best possible chance of building a life you love to live because you are specific. You are intentional. You have identified with pinpoint accuracy the destination that you want to land in this life.

While you are well on your way, this isn't the end. We have more work to do, but you should be very proud of yourself. If you've never identified what you want in life before, you now have crystal-clear clarity. You have a map that you should definitely hang on to, maybe even frame and hang up somewhere that you'll see every day. Make it the screensaver of your phone, put it in a book or on your desk. This will keep you focused on where you want to go in order to build a life you love to live.

The best way to do this is to begin living your plan out one step at a time, one day at a time. Steps lead to days, days become months, and months become years. Those years then become the life you love to live.

Vital Reflections to Discuss or Journal:

1. *Prior to reading this chapter, could you tell me what you truly wanted to accomplish in your life? How about now?*

2. *What do you want? Not what your parents want for you. Not what your spouse or kids want for you. What do YOU want most in this life? Is your answer the same as it's always been? Or has it changed over time?*

3. *Now that you have a life map to your destination/purpose, how can knowing exactly what you want in life benefit you on your journey?*

4. *Reflect on the lists you've made in this chapter. Now take each list and prioritize them in order of importance to you. They are all important, but which areas take precedence over the other? This will help you begin building your action plan.*

Chapter 10

THE KEY TO EVERYTHING

I can remember it like it was yesterday. The year was 2005. I had been working incredibly hard, and I was just about to graduate high school. I was able to save up enough money to purchase my very first car. I purchased this car from one of my very best friends, so I definitely got a great deal on it, but I was still proud, nonetheless. It was a 1996 Ford Taurus and it was purple as purple could be. My friends named this wonderful vehicle Purple Rain.

Purple Rain was great to me. She would go on to last me for years and years. Throughout that time, I took care of her; I got a little maintenance done here and there, including getting the oil changed. But here's something that I wanted to share with you. Don't judge me for this, but my car was due for an oil change one particular time. As normal, I planned to take it in to have this done. However, I realized once I checked my bank account that I did not have nearly as much money as I thought I did.

I thought to myself, 'How much do I really need an oil change anyway?' To be honest with you, I really had no idea why a car needed its oil changed to begin with. It was just something I did because I was told I needed to. I decided I needed the money a little bit more to survive. Surely an oil change can't be that important to a car as long as the engine stays intact, right? Everything else was good; my engine and transmission were fine, so I figured I was good to go.

I continued on, and after that I didn't think about it anymore. I kept driving my car without any problems. Before I knew it, I had driven about as many miles as was needed for another oil change. I was now two oil changes overdue, but at this point the thought of it was completely off my radar.

One day I was driving without a care in the world. I was completely oblivious. I was headed to my destination when it happened. Purple Rain's heart stopped, and that would be the last time I would ever drive her. See, what I didn't know was that oil changes were essential to the function of the engine of the car. I knew what I needed to do to my car. I knew I needed to get my oil changed. But I had no idea *why* I needed to do this. As a result, I ignored what was needed.

This leads to the next foundational pillar, and this is the hinge that the entire process hangs upon. The next pillar is understanding the why. I could go on and talk all day about the why, but I will attempt to keep this as short, sweet, and simple as possible, yet just as powerful and impactful, nevertheless. There are literally entire books written about the why. You just identified a beautiful map and a life vision for your own life. But, none of that matters a single bit if you don't understand *why* you want what you want.

The most detailed map can't physically take you to your destination, no matter how intricate, specific, or technologically advanced it is. To get there you need a vehicle that has the power to move. In this instance, your why is that vehicle that holds all the power to driving you to your destination in this life.

It's often been said that when your why is big enough, you can accomplish any what. As long as you know why, you will always learn how because life has a wonderful way of teaching you through all those lovely and not so lovely life experiences that we've been discussing in this book thus far. Over the next few paragraphs, I want to tell you about a few heroes who had tremendous whys, and because of this they were able to accomplish what sometimes seemed to be impossible.

William Kyle Carpenter is the youngest living soldier to ever be awarded the Medal of Honor. He received the nation's highest and most prestigious award for his outstanding bravery while on tour in Afghanistan. Carpenter shielded his friend from a hand grenade that was thrown onto the rooftop where they were stationed in November of 2010. Both men survived thanks to Kyle's actions.

Carpenter was 21at the time. Throwing his body onto a live grenade resulted in him losing most of his teeth and his right eye. His jaw was shattered, and his arm broken in numerous places. He has said that he doesn't remember the blast. Although there were no eyewitnesses, doctors have confirmed that his injuries were the result of his decision to throw himself on top of a grenade in order to shield his friend.

Kyle is an American hero. He was able to do what was needed to be done even in the most extreme of circumstances because he knew why he was doing what he was doing. It was due to the love he had for his country and the love for his friend and fellow soldier that allowed him to act so selflessly and heroically in a moment where it was needed most.

Martin Luther King Jr., is considered to be one of America's greatest orators. He was an activist and a humanitarian, as well as a devout Christian who believed that he could change the world through non-violent protest, which he did. He dedicated his life to overcoming racist policies which the government held in place at the time. He organized marches, parades, and campaigns against racial segregation.

In his famous "I Have a Dream" speech on August 28, 1963, King would say in part: "I have a dream that one day on the red hills of Georgia the sons of former slaves and the sons of former slave owners will be able to sit down together at the table of brotherhood... I have a dream that my four little children will one day live in a nation where they will not be judged by the color of their skin but by the content of their character." King was eventually assassinated because of his work in advancing the Civil Rights Campaign. He was killed for his determination to bring justice to people who were judged and horribly mistreated because of the color of their skin.

To this day King is considered an American hero, and even has a national holiday in his name. He not only knew what he was doing, but he understood why. He understood that his mission and his purpose was much bigger than himself. King understood that the ramifications could go on to transform the entire world. And not only could it change the world, it did change the world. And all because he understood why.

Oskar Schindler was a German industrialist who was part of the Nazi Party and is credited with saving the lives of over 1000 Jewish people. He did this by employing them in his factories in Poland, where he provided the army with enamel cookware.

Initially, his business was set up in order to make him a wealthy man. The Nazi regime that was in place allocated Jews a cheaper wage. That was his initial reason for hiring Jews.

This, however, changed when Schindler learned of the devastating goings on outside in the concentration camps. He then fought to protect as many Jewish people as he could. He bribed members of the Nazi Party with money and gifts so they would not harm his Jewish workers. After the war, he was in danger of being arrested as a criminal of war. He became bankrupt after spending all of his money on bribes for his employees. He later survived on donations sent to him from all over the world by the very Jews that he had saved during the war.

https://whatculture.com/offbeat/14-real-life-heroes-who-have-changed-the-world?page=6

Schindler is considered one of the greatest heroes in the history of the world. He was able to show extreme bravery in the midst of chaos, and because of this he saved the lives of many. He was able to do what he did because he understood the importance of showing mercy to his fellow man, regardless of race or religion. He was able to do this because he understood why.

All three of these gentlemen faced extreme circumstances through all odds and through the greatest adversities, even unto death. They were able to step up, stand up, and accomplish what was meant for them to accomplish because they understood why they were doing what they were doing. The why is pivotal. It's of the utmost importance.

So, my friend, it is not only imperative for you to know what you want and to have your map. You also need your drive, which is your why. You must know what you want, and you must know why you want it. The why is what will drive you to your what.

It's your why that keeps you going when you're down and your heart is hurting. It keeps you going when you're tired and your eyes have grown weary. When you are lost, lonely, or confused, it's your why that will keep you going toward your what. Sometimes you're faced with the utmost adversity and the biggest mountain to climb and you don't have any clue how you're going to make it through this situation to get to the next. It's in that moment that you look back to the very reason why you're doing what you were doing to begin with.

When you understand your personal why, hold it close to your heart. It will fill you up and give you the energy you need to keep going. Sometimes, the why is the only thing that can keep you going in those dark and trying times. It is your why that will propel you forward when the weariness and the weight of life begin to seem like more than you can bear. The why will give you the strength that you need to press on.

Now that you understand the importance of having a deeply convicting why, it's time to roll up your sleeves and get to work again. You have a vision in this life, but now you need to set up your vehicle to ensure that you get there, to ensure that you didn't just have an emotional and happy moment of celebration for no reason. This is to drive home the point of where you want to get to and to ensure that you make it to your destination.

You've already identified what you want in this life. This is your overall vision plan, what you want to accomplish. Now, on the next page, write down in a few sentences why you want to accomplish your vision plan. Don't think surface level. The deeper, the better.

After you've done this, you need to get more specific, just like you did in the previous chapter. List out the subcategories you had, including faith, family, finances, health and fitness, as well as any others you had. Now pinpoint and list why you want what you want in each one of those areas. Why do you want what you want in your faith walk, in your family life, in your finances, and in your health and fitness? Again, be as specific and honest as possible, and leave out anything that doesn't align with your overall why.

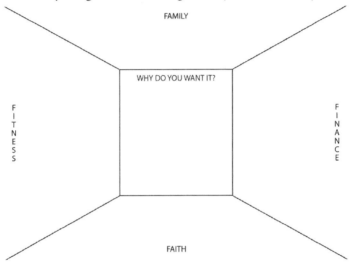

You've done it. Congratulations, my friend. Understanding and identifying this will give you fuel in every area of your life. Feelings can be deceiving and cloud your vision. But no matter what you're feeling externally, your why gives you the internal focus and drive you need to reach your destination. You will be able to press on because you've now identified the next foundational pillar of your entire life plan, the hinge that the entire process hangs upon. You have identified your why. You are now even farther along on your way to building a life that you love to live.

Vital Reflections to Discuss or Journal:

1. *What is the importance of knowing and understanding your why in life?*

2. *With as many details as possible, please list out your why. Take your time and think through your answer.*

3. *How can knowing your why in life benefit you on your journey?*

4. *Reflect on the lists you've made in this chapter. Now take each list and prioritize them in order of importance to you. They are all important, but which areas take precedence over the other? This will help sustain you as you execute your action plan.*

Chapter 11

WHAT ARE YOU LIVING FOR?

J oe Paterno was a staple of my childhood. For as long as I can remember, he was the head football coach of the Penn State Nittany Lions. He coached Penn State from 1966 until 2011, a whopping 45-year career. I don't know if I could imagine doing anything for 45 years. It's a struggle today for people to stay at a job longer than three years, let alone that many years. But his life centered around his work, the university, and the football program that he loved with all of his heart. With 409 victories, Paterno is the winningest coach in NCAA football history.

Unfortunately, nearing the end of his career, news shocked the entire world when it came out that one of his assistant coaches had been committing heinous acts against young men for many years. These acts went widely unreported. Thankfully, through counseling and healing, several young men were brave enough to stand up and speak out against the acts that were committed against them. The individual who committed these acts deserved to pay for what he did, and he is doing exactly that. He will spend the remainder of his life in jail.

This scandal led to a cloud that would hover over Paterno's legacy as the coach of Penn State. The head coach was fired by the Penn State Board of Trustees in a press conference on November 9, 2011 in State College, Pennsylvania. I cannot imagine what he must have felt after devoting the majority of his adult life towards this one role in this one job. It literally consumed everything around him. After leaving Penn State, Paterno quickly began suffering from health problems and was diagnosed with lung cancer in late 2011. On January 22, 2012, a mere 74 days after his firing, he succumbed to his illness and died at the age of 85.

The saddest part of his story is that it was later determined that he did not have a direct role in the events that took place with his assistant coach, and both his legacy and wins were reinstated at Penn State. Prior to his diagnosis of lung cancer, Paterno had no previous health issues. At the age of 84, he was still running up and down the sidelines, coaching with all the fire, fervor, and zest he had always had his entire career. But within just a few short months of losing his career, Paterno died. He died because he lost his reason to live.

This just goes to show you that without a reason to fight and a reason to live, it makes it very difficult for a person to go on. Oftentimes your reason to live is directly tied to your why, if it's not your actual why itself. You see this over and over again in many phases of life. One of the primary places you see this is with elderly couples. I can think of instance after instance where this has occurred.

One example is Herbert and Marilyn Frances DeLaigle. They met when she was 16 and he was 22 in Waynesboro,

Georgia. He asked Frances, as she was known, to marry him a year later. When Herbert's health started to decline in 2017, he scheduled a meeting with the preacher at his church. During the sit-down Herbert revealed that he wasn't afraid of dying at all, but he was scared to leave his beloved wife Frances behind.

After 71 years of marriage, Herbert and Frances DeLaigle died exactly 12 hours apart. Hebert died at the age of 94 from heart failure at 2:20am on July 12, 2018. Frances, 88, took her final breath at 2:20pm the same day. She had lost her reason to continue to fight and live. In the end, Frances was only without Herbert for 12 hours because it was all her heart could stand.

A 2013 study published in the Journal of Public Health followed 12,316 participants over the span of 10 years. The study found that people whose spouses have died have a 66 percent increased chance of dying themselves within the first three months following their spouse's death. It's a very real phenomenon, and it's not solely limited to the elderly. I've always wondered why this was the case.

Losing the will to live is often associated with a great loss. We all take losses in life and sometimes they can seem too much to bear. Unfortunately, there are some losses that are unfathomable, and words can't even express how to uplift you and encourage your heart after you've experienced a loss like that. Maybe you currently find yourself in a season of loss, which is why you struggled to figure out or answer the question of what your reason to live is.

Maybe you lost a career job after sacrificing many years of your life in the name of loyalty to your company. You poured out everything you had into the job, only to have it snatched away from you. And after that happens, maybe like Coach Joe Paterno, you find yourself wondering how you can even go on. Where do you even begin to start over after such a rewarding career?

Perhaps you're a parent that's grieving the loss of a child. There is nothing that can ever prepare you for that. On the flip side, perhaps you're a couple, and you've been trying again and again to have a child. But it just hasn't happened. You've struggled with infertility issues or maybe even lost precious babies through miscarriage, which affects so many couples today.

It may be that you've lost a relationship. You poured your entire soul into the well-being of another person, only to have them jerk the rug out from underneath you. Now you feel empty and lost without your soul mate. It could be that you've lost your home or your life savings due to some catastrophic event or major illness. You now find yourself struggling to have a will to fight, a will to go on.

All of these before-mentioned events are horrible, and I wish that I could reach out and take your pain away. But if I did this, I would rob you of your victory that comes at the end of your fight. Victory will be yours, that I'm sure of.

What I cannot tell you is how long the night will last. What I can tell you is that the night will not last forever and the sun will shine on your life again. Even when you feel weary, your heart is heavy, and it doesn't feel like you have a reason to press on, there is always a reason to keep going. You have a reason to live. Stick with me and I'll help you find exactly what your reason to live is.

Just as people without anything to live for tend to have shorter life expectancies, people that have something to live for typically have longer life expectancies. You hear this all the time. People all over the world in the worst of circumstances and the darkest of times survive against all odds. They do this because they had a reason to live. They had something on their conscious mind that gave them the strength they needed to fight in the most inopportune and adverse situations you could think of.

One such situation comes to mind right now of a warrior friend of mine. Astin Curry was a young woman on a mission to live her most abundant and good life. Thriving in many different areas, she was living life and truly loving it. She had her beautiful baby girl, and after this it seemed as if things couldn't get more wonderful, beautiful, or perfect in her life.

And then that harrowing day would come. A day that no one could be prepared for. A day where she was diagnosed with breast cancer. I remember watching her share her thoughts, feelings, and emotions after receiving this news. She shared how scary and painful it was to receive the diagnosis, and there were tears in her eyes as she considered the possibilities of what could come. We've all seen it happen too many times. Far too many good people's lives have been taken far too soon from the evil monster that is cancer.

But I remember seeing something shift in her mind one day. Astin knew that she had many reasons to live, and among the greatest of these reasons was her beautiful baby girl. So, she dug in with all the fervor inside of her and she fought. She fought through the entire process: the chemo, the sickness, the agony, and the pain. She was determined in her mind that she would not lose the battle to cancer, and she didn't.

I'll never forget the day she announced that she was in full remission and cancer free. It was an amazingly joyous occasion. I celebrated with her as if I had received the news myself. After that, life continued to go on. We all went back to life as we knew it. But then lightening, as it never typically does, struck twice.

I was on social media, and once again I saw tear-filled eyes as Astin shared that the monster she had fought so hard to defeat had decided to come back for round two. Just a few short years after beating it, she received her second diagnosis of breast cancer, all before age 30. This time, however, I remember seeing something that was different. From early on in the process, there was a strength and a will to fight in her. There was a level of courage and indescribable bravery.

Astin's fight even built me up and lifted me up. What did I have to complain about? If she was ready to stand and fight for her life, what was I doing sitting around and moping about small things? I watched this young woman step up as the hero that she is, battle with everything inside of her, and fight this evil sickness off again for the second time. And then it happened. There was another momentous occasion and joyous celebration as she announced to the world for the second time that her cancer was in remission once again.

Just because she triumphed doesn't mean there weren't hard days. Throughout her journey, I prayed for Astin and sent her several messages of encouragement to try to uplift her during her battle. You never know where a person is or how badly they might need a boost of support. Anytime you feel it on your heart, I encourage you to follow through with that feeling. Send a message of encouragement or just let the person know you're thinking of them. That's exactly what I did, and I hope I was able to make Astin's journey a little bit easier.

Watching her overcome this monster again is one of the greatest triumphs I've ever seen. And you know why she was able to do it? Because every time she thought about the beautiful life that she had created, her beloved daughter, Astin had a reason to live. All she could think about was not wanting to leave her in this world without a mommy, without the love and nurturing care of a supportive mom. So, she fought with everything inside of her to push this illness back for the second time.

She would not be defeated. When you have something to live for, nothing will stop you from fighting for your life with everything you have. Astin refused to give up because she definitely had something to live for. Now she's a very serious advocate for breast cancer awareness, early detection, coping, and treatment. She has even more to live for as she spreads her message of love and positivity through her organization Love While You Cancer.

My question for you today is: which one are you? We've heard several stories of people who through life and circumstances lost their will to live. But we've also heard a story of a person with incredible will and a reason to live. Where do you find yourself? Are you still asleep? Are you going through the motions while life passes you by, or are you sincerely ready to truly take back control of the wheel of your life so that you can live in the abundance that was planned out for you in the beginning?

If you're still alive and breathing, pause for a moment. Breathe in slowly. Exhale. Breathe out. Do you feel that? That means you're here. You are alive, and there is great purpose inside of you. As long as that is still the case, no matter how bad, ugly, or negative things seem, there is a reason for you to press on. You have something to live for. Don't believe me? Let me show you.

I think of some of the greatest movies I've ever seen in my life. Consider the greatest stories ever told. I'm not saying these are the greatest movies of all time, but in a list of the top 25 these would both definitely be there. They may even be in the top 10. I'm talking about *The Lord of the Rings* trilogy. Or you could even even insert the Harry Potter movies here. And, spoiler alert! If you continue reading at this point and you haven't seen those movies, I may give away some major plotlines.

Here we go. *The Lord of the Rings* is three very incredible, epic stories all in one compilation. They tell you a miraculous tale of triumph and victory, but what if the author had decided to end the story at the end of the second book? What would have happened to the hero of our story? What would have happened to Mr. Baggins or his friend? What would have happened to the ring itself? There would be so many questions left unanswered. There would be so much hurt, so much pain, and so much death. It wouldn't be the story that we understand and love today.

Similarly, with Harry Potter, what would happen if J.K. Rowling decided after four or five books to end the story? It's a seven-book story, but there are eight movies as the final book is broken into two movies. Let's say she ended the story at the end of the seventh movie. I won't give details, but this is not a great time to end that story. We all know about cliffhangers, and that would have been the ultimate cliffhanger. Nobody likes cliffhangers because there is no peace in your life. There is no resolve. Everything feels off, as if something is missing.

That is the case for your life as well, my friend. These stories weren't considered some of the greatest volumes of work of all time until their completion. And as long as you're still alive, you have not reached the end of your story. As the hero, yeah, you've gone through some major adversities. Maybe you've taken a lot of losses, but you've had some wins along the way as well. It's hard, though, and you're figuring it out as you go. Unfortunately, life doesn't come with a manual, and what you're left with is a lot of people doing the best they can to try to make the most of the time that they have in this world.

My sincerest advice to you is to choose life. I'll say that again. Choose life because someone somewhere in this world is suffering just a little bit more than you are and they don't see a way out. They don't see any possibility of a positive outcome. They've given up all hope. In all of your mess you may be the very solution to their problems. Your past pain and the experiences that you've had, good, bad and ugly, make you real. They make you relatable. And hearing the way that you made it through may be just the antidote they need to survive.

Furthermore, think of all the little things in this world you enjoy. Sometimes when our brains get so focused on the things that are plaguing us and pulling us down, we lose sight of those simple pleasures. For me, I love being near any body of water and hearing the soothing sounds of water gently crashing against the shore. Any type of waves or falling water brings peace to my life. That's a little thing.

I also love the smell of fresh breakfast, of bacon and eggs cooking in the kitchen on an early weekend morning. I enjoy the feel of a cool breeze smacking against my face as I look at the colorful leaves during my favorite season of autumn. These are all small, simple things that bring me joy. You have little things that you love as well. You have big things that you're hoping for, but you have small pleasures, as well. Never take those for granted.

You owe it to yourself to stay tuned to see how your story ends. If life has taught me anything at all - and believe me, it's taught me a lot - it's that at any given moment you are only one choice away, you are only one connection away, you're only one unexpected blessing in your favor away from transforming your entire life. You live, so that in itself is a reason to hold on. You never know when your circumstances are going to flip upside down. Don't give up on yourself or your life. Don't throw in the towel just because it's a little tough right now when you still have reasons to live.

I live in the great state of Oklahoma where quite literally when it rains, it pours. We have an insane storm season, also known as tornado season. Although it lasts year-round, prime conditions are typically late March through August. When storms come, they are very scary. It gets incredibly dark and the wind often blows hard enough to snap young to middle-aged trees in half. It's imperative to understand, though, that even in that season, in the midst of the worst storm you can imagine, it's still temporary. My encouragement to you is that this too shall pass.

You don't throw away an entire house just because it's being rained on. Nor should you give up on your entire life and all the possibilities that come with it because your present reality is cold, dark, and wet from being rained on. Whatever you do, never give up on yourself. Remember, up to this point, you've made it through every impossible situation you've ever faced. Time after time after time, and you're still living to tell the story. So that's exactly what I want you to do.

Over the last couple of chapters, we've spent some intense time discovering what you want out of this life and why you want it. This next step will help bring even further clarity to your why which is so important for you accomplishing your goals. This is what I want you to do. It's time to create your life mission statement. Many of us have heard of mission statements before and they can sometimes be difficult to come up with. All you have to do is search the internet and you'll come up with hundreds of results on how to write your own.

But I want to give you a simple formula that you can do right now to help you determine and write down your life mission statement. You can take this as deep as you want to. Keep in mind, you're not locked into what you decide on today, but you need to have something because this will be your reason to continue. Just like your why, your reason to live which is tied to that will bring crystal-clear clarity about what you want. It will help propel you into the life that you love to live.

This is what I want you to do. It's as simple as this. Write down, "I want _____," then write down what you want in that blank. Continue on with, "in order to _____," and fill in this blank with why you want what you want. Finish with, "so that _____," which is where you write the result of what you want and why you want it. What do you want the end result to be? And that there, my friend, that simple, is your life mission statement. The end result will look like this:

"I want _____ in order to _____, so that _____."

Once you have this, you should keep it close to you. Where you did or did not believe you have a reason to keep going, now you know without a shadow of doubt that you do. There in a nutshell is your reason to press on and continue making the most of your journey in this life. Even if you still don't fully believe how valuable you are, you have to keep trusting the words I've shared with you and do your very best to execute your action plan. I heard a wise person say, "you can't feel your way into an action, but you can act your way into a feeling". Cling to those words you've written and hold them near and dear to your heart. They will hold you up, motivate, and inspire you to keep pressing on both in the best and the worst of times. Hold on, my friend. The best in your life is still yet to come. Now that you have crystal-clear clarity and a perfectly clear plan, you're on the way. It's time to execute your vision plan and live out your purpose in this life. Why? Because YOU CAN!

Vital Reflections to Discuss or Journal:

1. *What stood out to you from this chapter?*

2. *Have you ever lost someone or something of great value to you? How did you overcome the deep grief in your heart?*

3. *What are you living for? What gives you the strength to keep fighting for your life even on your worst days?*

4. *Have you ever had a vision plan for your life before?*

5. *Now that you have a crystal-clear plan, how do you plan to keep it in front of you so that you remain focused and never fall asleep at the wheel of your life again?*

Chapter 12

ANCHORED

L ife has not been a cakewalk or simple walk in the park. There have been a lot of grueling battles along the way that have led me to this very moment. I've taken a lot of knocks and been cut down. I've been spit on, and I've been slandered. I've had sickness, hurt, and heartbreak. I've experienced loss and unimaginable suffering. I could go on and on, but what's most important to note is that I have lived.

I have countless stories of the storms that I have faced in my life. There's the story that I've already shared with you about suffering from major anxiety as a young child, far younger than anyone should, and how it still haunts me to this very day. I had close loved ones who would mock me, belittle me, and insult my intelligence and my character. This caused an unimaginable pain from the very people that you want and expect to love you most.

I've experienced hunger pain while desperately wishing to have something to eat. I could tell you about the days of our childhood, watching my parents struggle and fight and do the very best they could to stay afloat, yet still not having enough to handle all of the crises that life brought our way. I remember my mom putting box-fan units in the windows during the summertime when it was 100 degrees. She would go outside every hour on the hour at night just to turn on the water hose to spray water into those fans so they would blow a little mist on us to cool down the room at night.

The stories go on and on. There was the time I lost a very close childhood friend. When this happened, my entire community was rocked at tragically having a life lost far too soon. The fact that it happened so unexpectedly made matters worse. This left an unthinkable ache and pain on all of us.

I went to college at a school 500 miles away from home in the great state of Texas. At one point, through a series of unfortunate events, I was unfairly and unjustly accused of something and not allowed to enter campus. I had nowhere to go and my mom didn't have money to send to me. I had to make the difficult choice to go into the unsafe confines in the middle of town to a laundromat. I locked my doors, laid my seat back, and slept in my car, desperately hoping that no one would come and kick in my doors and rob me, which wasn't uncommon in the area I was in.

One of my lowest moments was when my wife and I didn't have a car of our own. We had to share a vehicle that a church member was kind enough to allow us to use. It wasn't the nicest looking car, but it ran. The sunroof had been destroyed by Oklahoma hailstorms. There were days that it would rain unexpectedly, and I was totally unprepared. I recall driving to work wearing a suit and being rained on.

During this difficult season, my wife and I were still newlyweds. I was working at a company through a temporary agency when I was called into the office. I was informed that due to budget cuts they had to let me go. My things were packed into a Walmart bag, handed to me, and I was escorted from the building. My wife had the vehicle this particular day because she had mandatory meetings she had to attend. Since she couldn't be pulled away from the meetings, I proceeded to leave with no ride. I walked down the street on a hot summer day, wearing a suit, sweating profusely, and not knowing how we would survive with the bills that were mounting.

If you've ever experienced the loss of a job or any unexpected absence from work for a prolonged period of time, you know as well as I do that although income ceases, bills and responsibilities do not. They continue to pile and stack up. I remember eviction notices on my door with a five-day notice to exit the premises or be taken to court. I'll never forget my wife's large eyes looking up at me, asking how we would survive.

I could go on with stories of all of my valley lows, of all of the struggles, hurt, pain, and grief that life has hit me with. You may be wondering; how does one go on? How does one find their reason to live and press through adverse situations of the magnitude that I've just shared? I'm glad we've come to this point because there were times in my own life where I wondered how I would go on.

I've learned something interesting over the course of my life. I'll shy away from my airplane analogy at this time and give you a new one. This one has to do with ships. One of the most incredible things about ships is how they function. There's a special device built inside of them as a safety mechanism called an anchor. Anchors are large, heavy devices typically made out of steel, attached by a chain on large ships and possibly rope on smaller ships. They're created to drop deep down under the water into the seabed and hook onto something.

This is significant for this reason: in life, no one can ever promise you that storms won't come. No one can promise that you won't face extreme grief, that you won't experience the loss of a loved one far before you could ever be prepared or ready. It's not guaranteed that you will always have an abundance of money at your disposal. You don't know if you'll go through financial hardships and have to wonder how you're going to make ends meet. No one can assure you that your children won't fall into extreme situations or trouble. They could be bullied, belittled, or even worse, harmed or significantly hurt.

No one can promise you that the storms in life won't come and completely rock your world, just as the hurricanes and other massive storms rock large boats in the ocean. But just like those ships, it is incredibly important to be anchored. In the middle of storms and extreme circumstance, the anchor is able to keep the ship grounded so that it doesn't blow away or find itself too far off its course, crashed and lost forever. The beauty of the anchor is this: it doesn't lock the ship so tightly that it's in prison. It doesn't keep the ship from moving, from feeling the wind and the massive waves crashing into it. It doesn't prevent any of this. What is does do, however, is keep the ship from floating away into the abyss for good. It protects it in the midst of the storm.

You may ask, how was I able to survive? How am I able to keep a smile on my face every single day whether it be in a classroom, on a job, in church, or just in front of people? No matter where I am, I'm always giving life, love, and spreading joy and positivity. When you ask me how I'm able to do this in the face of the most extreme circumstances, it is because I am anchored. I have an anchor, my friend, and His name is Jesus Christ.

You see, in every situation I've ever been through, through all the hurt and pain every single time, and even now when adversity comes my way, I'm reminded of Scriptures all throughout the Good Book. You ever heard of this book? It's called the Bible, and it's God's inspired Word. I believe it with all my heart. In this book, there are so many uplifting words written by men and women who walked the earth long before me. There are passages of Scripture that tell me things such as, "Count it all joy" when you fall into horrible situations. One may ask, 'How do you do that? How does one count anything joy when you're in the midst of the most frustrating seasons of your life?'

The way that you do that is through your heart, your mind, and your soul being anchored. Being anchored to Jesus doesn't come without misconceptions at times, though. A lot of people get caught up. They make a choice and give their heart to Christ, only to find out that life still hits. Adversity still comes. The wind and the waves continue to come crashing, and the rain still beats you down as if there was no shelter in sight. This causes you to wonder... what is the point? What am I even doing this for? Why am I even wasting my time believing?

I'll tell you the point. The Scriptures never promised that you wouldn't feel the rain, that you wouldn't feel the storm. That's what makes you human. That's what makes your experience relevant. What the Bible does tell you is that in the midst of your worst storm, you won't be alone. Sometimes you can't see to the other side and you're literally fearing for your safety and your life. You feel anxious, have a nervous feeling in the pit of your stomach, and worry begins to completely overshadow your mind.

When you find yourself in these places, you can take comfort when you have an anchor. It doesn't matter if life moves, shakes, and begins to blow you. It's okay if it begins to move you and press you a little bit out of your comfort zone, off your perch of comfortability. You can rest assured and take solace. You can find peace in the depths of your heart by knowing that you are anchored. Even though you might feel discomfort, you will not be harmed. You will not blow away because you are anchored.

There were countless situations in my life that I should never have made it out of. Some were situations I should never have been in in the first place. And some were situations that people would say it's not humanly possible for me to continue to walk with a smile on my face. The only thing I can tell you is it's because I'm anchored to Jesus.

The big question for you now is: are you anchored? And if so, what are you anchored to? I am not telling you that you have to make the choice to be anchored the way that I am. I'm not trying to force you in any way, shape, form, or fashion to choose my anchor. But this is what I can tell you. If you don't have an anchor, it is a recipe for disaster.

Many times, you may have found yourself questioning and wondering: what's the point in going on? You may have even asked yourself if you have a reason to live. Maybe you've woken up and not recognized yourself when you looked in the mirror, not recognized the life that you're living because you found yourself so far off track that you don't even know where to begin to find your way back. This means you've been without an anchor.

With an anchor, even when you drift a little, you never go too far. You're always within distance of your solid foundation. If you are not anchored, what I urge you to do is to find an anchor for your life. If you don't, you'll forever be asleep at the wheel. You'll never wake up, and you'll find yourself constantly struggling unnecessarily without reason. There's no reason for you to be drifting when you have the ability to choose an anchor. In this life, the anchor is the difference maker.

It would be a tragedy for me to write this entire book and to leave out something that's such a large part of my life. Every storm I've ever faced, I've never had to be fully worried. Even that day I found myself walking down the highway with no job, no car, no money, and not knowing how we were going to pay rent I still felt an indescribable peace in my soul. And that is because of who I am anchored to. From the very depths of my soul, what I want is for you to feel that same type of peace. I want you to know what it feels like to be loved unconditionally no matter what you do. That is what I get from my anchor who is Jesus Christ.

Sadly, many people won't even have a conversation about Jesus. I believe it's because the world has done a horrible job of presenting Him and making Him out to be something He's not. But my Bible teaches me that Jesus Christ is love, and He came to earth so that He can give us life. So that whenever you find yourself alone, crying yourself to sleep, at the end of your rope and feeling like all hope is lost and there's nothing to be joyful about, you can find peace and comfort in His presence instead.

I want you to know that when you feel like no one else in this world loves you, Jesus Christ loves you. I know this for fact. I believe it with every fiber in my body. As a friend of yours, you should want me to share this good news with you. And we are friends now. You've heard enough stories about me and my life and read these words long enough to know that we're on a different level now. As your friend, I don't share this with the intention of trying to persuade you or force you into believing something different than what you believe. I share this to let you know what the difference has been in my own life. I share this so you can see the benefits of making sure your own life is anchored in whichever way you choose.

I get asked every so often, almost on a monthly basis, how do you always smile? How do you smile when I know deep down your soul is hurting and wanting to cry out? The answer is my anchor. How do you have hope when all around it seems hopeless? The answer is my anchor. How do you keep from being blown and washed away from all the different ideas that are presented in the world today? From seeing all the hurt and pain? Seeing races turn against one another and ready to jump at each other's throat? Watching friends that I've sat at the dinner table with become massive enemies over a political standpoint or even a National Football League team? When we should be loving people, how do you continue to stand? How do you walk with strength, dignity, and the joy that rests on your life? The answer is always my anchor.

The reality is, I made a choice long ago to submit my heart fully to Jesus Christ and devote my life to giving life and giving love on His behalf, and my life was spared in that accident on the highway. I shouldn't be here. After a season of wondering why I was still here I made a promise. I made a promise to God that I would spend the remainder of my days giving life, giving love, and pouring my all into every single human being on His behalf. So, my prayer for you is that you would realize, if nothing else, that there is a God in heaven who loves you.

My favorite passage of Scripture is from John chapter 6. Jesus was speaking and began to cry out in verses 38-39: "For I have come down from heaven not to do my will but to do the will of him who sent me. And this is the will of him who sent me, that I shall lose none of all those he has given me but raise them up at the last day." That's the man I'm anchored to. John 3:16 says God loved the world so much that He sacrificially paid the ultimate sacrifice and gave His only son so that the world would not perish but have life eternally. That's my anchor. That's the person I'm anchored to and that my life is devoted to.

That's another part of my why that keeps me going. When I don't feel like it and feel like giving up, my life vision plan is centered around an anchor that keeps me grounded. My anchor keeps me focused, faithful, hopeful, uplifted, and alive. And I know it can do the same thing for you, my friend.

As you get ready to enter into the next phase of your life, this is what I know. If you take these steps seriously, really sit down and spend the time, you can now answer what you want in this life and know exactly why you want it. You have a reason to live, and you need to find something to tie that to with an anchor. If you do this, I can promise you that no matter what life throws your way, you will always come out on top. You will still be standing. Your story is still being written, and the pen is in your hand. You are the master ready to create the masterpiece that is your life, and I can't wait to watch you do it.

You owe it to yourself from this very moment. I want you to promise yourself right now that you won't ever settle for anything less than what you know is your very best. That no matter what naysayers say you will realize the specialness and uniqueness that is you. That regardless of what those people who judge, mock, envy, and belittle you, you will understand that you were created on this earth with great purpose to accomplish something that only you can accomplish. There's not another soul on the entire planet who can replace you and your purpose in this world.

I want you to commit to a few moments a day of daily affirmations. Remember to tell yourself how special you are. Tell yourself how smart, wonderful, and intelligent you are. Make your affirmations unique. Build and uplift yourself. Pour into yourself. Stop investing in everything else except for yourself. And remember to always stay focused on the map to your journey and your destination.

I can't promise you that there will be no bad days. What I can promise you, however, is that if you cling to these principles, hang on to this method and formula, and stay committed to the vision for your life that we've just unfolded, laid down, and put on paper, you will have more good days than bad. You will reach your destination. It's time to truly live and love life. Why, you ask? Because you can!

Vital Reflections to Discuss or Journal:

1. *Reflect on your life. What are some of your worst experiences you've ever had? How did you handle them? What sustained you during these difficult times?*

2. *Have you ever felt as if you weren't in control of your own circumstances? How did this make you feel?*

3. *Do you have an anchor in this life? If not, why not? If so, write it down as a reminder that you are safe the next time there's a storm.*

4. *How will you implement the knowledge, insights, and plans that you've gained throughout this book to help you build a life you truly love living?*

5. *Who do you know that desperately needs this book? Please tell them about it and how it helped you.*

ABOUT THE AUTHOR,

Marcus Black is a former pastor of many years and current urban missionary. He provides leadership and mentoring programs to several inner-city schools.

He's a traveling inspirational speaker, life coach, and host of The Vitalize Podcast.

Ever since he nearly lost his life at age 18, he's been committed to making the most of every moment given to him on this earth! Not only does he want to live life to the fullest, but he also wants to give wisdom, love, life, and energy to you and all those he comes into contact with along his journey! That's the driving force behind his movement; The Vitalize Project!

Learn more about his work and services at mblackspeaks. com

Made in the USA
Columbia, SC
08 June 2021